DISABLING
PROFESSIONS

ABOUT THE SERIES

IDEAS IN PROGRESS is a commercially published series of working papers dealing with alternatives to industrial society. It is our belief that the ills and profound frustrations which have overtaken man are not merely due to industrial civilization's inadequate planning and faulty execution, but are caused by fundamental errors in our basic thinking about goals. This series is designed to question and rethink the underlying concepts of many of our institutions and to propose alternatives. Unless this is done soon society will undoubtedly create even greater injustices and inequalities than at present. It is to correct this trend that authors are invited to submit short texts of work in progress of interest not only to their colleagues but also to the general public. The series fosters direct contact between the author and the reader. It provides the author with the opportunity to give wide circulation to his draft while he is still developing an idea. It offers the reader an opportunity to participate critically in shaping this idea before it has taken on a definite form. Readers are invited to write directly to the authors of the present volume at the following address:

Ivan Illich, Apdo. 479, Cuernavaca, Mexico.

Irving Kenneth Zola, Department of Sociology,
Brandeis University, Waltham, Mass. 02145

John McKnight, Centre for Urban Affairs,
Northwestern University, Evanstan, Illinois 60201

Jonathan Caplan, 2 Belsize Mews, Belsize Lane,
London NW3 5AT

Harley Shaiken, 18285 Birchcrest, Detroit, Michigan 48221

ABOUT THE AUTHORS

IVAN ILLICH was born in 1926. He studied theology, philosophy and history. He was assistant pastor in an Irish-Puerto Rican parish in New York and vice-rector of the Catholic University of Puerto Rico. From 1962-1976 he directed research seminars at CIDOC in Cuernavaca where he still lives. He is the author of *Celebration of Awareness, Deschooling Society, Energy & Equity, Limits to Medicine: Medical Nemesis – The Expropriation of Health, The Right to Useful Unemployment, Gender* and *H_2O and the Waters of Forgetfulness*.

IRVING KENNETH ZOLA was born in 1935. He studied history and sociology and taught at Harvard University before becoming Professor of Sociology at Brandeis University. His special subject is Medical Sociology and he has published widely on that subject in the United States and Europe.

JOHN McKNIGHT was born in 1931. Formerly working in Civil Rights and Civil Liberties he is now Professor of Communications Studies and Urban Affairs at Northwestern University in Chicago. He has lectured in the United States, Europe and Latin America and has published many articles on social work.

JONATHAN CAPLAN was born in 1951. After reading law at Downing College, Cambridge, he became a scholar of Gray's Inn, London. He has worked in the United States for the BBC and contributes articles and legal features to a number of national newspapers and periodicals. He is now a practicing lawyer. With Christopher Price he is the co-author of *The Confait Confessions*.

HARLEY SHAIKEN was born in 1946. He abandoned his studies at the University of Chicago because 'I felt that my studies lacked relevance to either my background or the world I saw around me'. He worked first as an unskilled worker and then took an 8,000 hour Machine Repair Apprenticeship at General Motors in Detroit. He has worked two years in a steel mill, five years for a large car manufacturer and five years in a small machine shop. He now teaches at the Massachusetts Institute of Technology.

Ideas in Progress

DISABLING
PROFESSIONS

**Ivan Illich
Irving Kenneth Zola   John McKnight
Jonathan Caplan   Harley Shaiken**

**Marion Boyars
New York · London**

First published Great Britain in 1977
Reprinted 1978
Republished in 1987
Reprinted 1992
by Marion Boyars Publishers
24 Lacy Road, London SW15 1NL
237 East 39th Street, New York, NY 10016

Distributed in the United States and Canada by
Rizzoli International Publications Inc, New York

Distributed in Australia by
Peribo Pty Ltd., Terrey Hills, N.S.W. 2084

British Library Cataloguing in Publication Data
Data available

Library of Congress Cataloging in Publication Data

Disabling professions.
　(Ideas in progress)
　1. Professions — Social aspects.　I. Illich, Ivan,
1926–　　　II. Series.
HT687.D57　1987　　　305.5′53　　　87–6558

ISBN 0–7145–2510–3 (pbk.)

Printed and bound in Great Britain by
Itchen Printers Ltd., Southampton.

CONTENTS

The professionals, that is the skilled and learned experts who apply their knowledge to the affairs and in the service of others, are traditionally held in high esteem. For generations, divinity, the law, medicine and even the military and now the newer professions in the fields of education, welfare, architecture, industrial management etc. have been acknowledged as being selflessly devoted to the good of the weaker and less knowledgeable members of society, thus enabling those who lack the capacity to fend for themselves to lead fuller, safer and healthier lives. However, the question must now be asked whether the professions in fact provide their services so altruistically, and whether we are really enriched and not just subordinated by their activities. There is a growing awareness that during the past twenty years or so, the professions have gained a supreme ascendency over our social aspirations and behaviour by tightly organizing and institutionalizing themselves. At the same time we have become a virtually passive clientèle: dependent, cajoled and harrassed, economically deprived and physically and mentally damaged by the very agents whose raison d'être it is to help.

But the debate about the beneficence of the professions must not express itself merely in vague frustrations. We must make an organized attempt to understand what the professions' power consist of and by what they are motivated. And we must examine the nature of our own submission to the professions' disabling effects, now and in the future. This symposium, whose contributors are as disparate as as social philosopher and factory worker, presents, as is the the intention of the *Ideas in Progress* series, a true parliament of ideas: it analyzes and traces the history of professional power in many fields; it demonstrates specific disabilities which have been created by modern professions; it pinpoints the political dangers of oligarchic and self-appointed élitist institutions, and it sounds a clarion call for professionals to stop making a monopoly of their vocations and for people to be more discriminating in their choice of alternatives.

Each of the essays provides a basis for the author to expand his ideas and solutions into a fuller treatment at a future occasion. It is hoped that readers will avail themselves of the opportunity given in this publication to enter into the debate by accepting the invitation to communicate with the authors and to express their views, hopefully as much in disagreement as in agreement.

THE PUBLISHERS

IVAN ILLICH

Disabling Professions

One way to close an age is to give it a name that sticks. I propose that we name the mid-twentieth century The Age of Disabling Professions, an age when people had "problems", experts had "solutions" and scientists measured imponderables such as "abilities" and "needs". This age is now at an end, just as the age of energy splurges has ended. The illusions that made both ages possible are increasingly visible to common sense. But no public choice has yet been made. Social acceptance of the illusion of professional omniscience and omnipotence may result either in compulsory political creeds (with their accompanying versions of a new fascism), or in yet another historical emergence of neo-Promethean but essentially ephemeral follies. Informed choice requires that we examine the specific role of the professions in determining who got what from whom and why, in this age.

To see the present clearly, let us imagine the children who will soon play in the ruins of school buildings, air terminals and hospitals. In these concrete castles turned cathedrals, built to protect us against ignorance, discomfort, pain and death, the children of tomorrow will reenact in their play the delusions of our Age of Professions, as from ancient castles and cathedrals we reconstruct today the crusades of knights against sin and Turk in the Age of Faith. Children in their games will mingle the uniquack which now pollutes our language with archaisms inherited from robber barons and cowboys. I see them addressing each other as chairman and secretary rather than as chief and lord. Even now some adults have the grace to blush when they slip into managerial pidgin English with terms such as policy-making, social planning and problem-solving.

The Age of Professions will be remembered as the time when politics withered, when voters, guided by professors, entrusted to technocrats the power to legislate needs, renounced the authority to decide who needs what and suffered monopolistic oligarchies to determine the means by which these needs shall be met. It will be remembered as the age of schooling, when people for one-third of their lives had their learning needs prescribed and were trained how to accumulate further needs, and for the other two-thirds became clients of prestigious pushers who managed their habits. It will be remembered as the age when recreational travel meant a packaged gawk at strangers, and intimacy meant following the sexual rules laid down by Masters and Johnson and their kin; when formed opinion was a replay of last night's TV talk-show, and voting the approval of persuaders and salesmen for more of the same.

Future students will be as much confused by the supposed differences between capitalist and socialist professional institutions as today's students are by the claimed differences between late Reformation Christian sects. They will discover that the professional librarians, surgeons, or supermarket-designers in poor and/or socialist countries towards the end of each decade came to keep the same records, used the same tools, built the same spaces that their colleagues in rich countries had pioneered at the decade's beginning. Archeologists will label the ages of our lifespan not by potsherds but by professional fashions, reflected in the mod-trends of UN publications.

It would be pretentious to predict if this age, when needs were shaped by professional design, will be remembered with a smile or with a curse. I do, of course, hope that it will be remembered as the night when father went on a binge, dissipated the family fortune, and obligated the children to start anew. Sadly, and much more probably, it will be remembered as the age when a whole generation's frenzied pursuit of impoverishing wealth rendered all freedoms alienable and, after first turning politics into the organized gripes of welfare-recipients, extinguished itself in a benign totalitarianism. I consider such a descent into techno-fascism as unavoidable unless the major thrust of social criticism begins to change from the support of a new or radical professionalism into the endorsement of a patronizing and sceptical attitude towards the experts—especially when they presume to diagnose and to prescribe. As technology is blamed for environmental degradation, the complaint may be turned into a demand that engineers ought to study biology. As long as hospital catastrophes are blamed on the rapacious doctor or the negligent nurse, the question of whether the patient can in principle benefit from hospitalization is never raised. If mere capitalist gain is blamed for an economics of inequality, industrial standardization and concentration—causing an unequal power structure—will be left uncriticized and unchanged.

Only if we understand the way in which dependence on commodities has legitimized wants, coined them urgent and exasperated needs while simultaneously destroying people's ability to fend for themselves, can the progress into a new dark age be avoided, an age in which masturbatory self-indulgence might be the safest assertion of independence. Only if our culture's market intensity is systematically exposed as the source of its deepest built-in frustrations will we stop the current perversion of research, ecological concern and the class struggle itself. Presently, these activities are principally in the service of an increased servitude of people to commodities.

The return to an era that fosters participatory

politics in which needs are defined by general consent is hampered by an obstacle that is both brittle and unexamined: the role that a new kind of professional élite plays in validating the world-wide religion that promotes impoverishing greed. It is therefore necessary that we clearly understand, 1) the nature of professional dominance, 2) the effects of professional establishment, 3) the characteristics of imputed needs and 4) the illusions which have enslaved us to professional management.

DOMINANT PROFESSIONS

Let us first face the fact that the bodies of specialists that now dominate the creation, adjudication and implementation of needs are a new kind of cartel. They are more deeply entrenched than a Byzantine bureaucracy, more international than a world church, more stable than any labour union, endowed with wider competencies than any shaman, and equipped with a tighter hold over those they claim as victims than any mafia.

The new organized specialists must, though, be carefully distinguished from racketeers. Educators, for instance, now tell society what must be learned, and are in a position to write off as valueless what has been learned outside of school. By establishing this kind of monopoly that enables them to preclude you from shopping elsewhere and from making your own booze, they at first seem to fit the dictionary definition of gangsters. But gangsters, for their own profit, corner a basic necessity by controlling supplies. Today, doctors and social workers—as formerly only priests and jurists—gain legal power to create the need that, by law, they alone will be allowed to satisfy. Unlike yesterday's liberal professions that provided ethical backing for high-status hawkers, the new dominant professions claim control over human needs, *tout court*. They turn the modern state into a holding corporation of enterprises which facilitates the operation of their self-certified competencies: equal needs are laid on the citizen/client, only to be fulfilled in a zero-sum game.

Control over work is not a new development. Professionalism is one of many forms that the control over work has taken. In former times soldiers of fortune refused to fight until they got the licence to plunder. Lysistrata organized female chattel to enforce peace by refusing sex. Doctors in Cos conspired by oath to pass trade secrets only to their offspring. Guilds set the curriculum, prayers, tests, pilgrimages and hazings through which Hans Sachs had to pass before he was permitted to shoe his fellow burghers. In capitalist countries, unions attempt to control who shall work what hours for what minimum pay. All trade associations are attempts by those who sell their labour to determine how work shall be done, and by whom. Professions also do this, but they go further: they decide what shall be made, for whom and how their decrees shall be enforced. They claim special, incommunicable authority to determine not just the way things are to be made, but also the reason why their services are mandatory. Many professions are now so highly developed that they not only exercise tutelage over the citizen-become-client, but also determine the shape of his world-become-ward.]

There is a further distinction between professional power and that of other occupations. Its authority springs from a different source: a guild, a union or a gang forces respect for its interest and rights by strike, blackmail or overt violence. A profession, like a priesthood, holds power by concession from an élite whose interests it props up. As a priesthood provides eternal salvation, so a profession claims legitimacy as the interpreter, protector and supplier of a special, this-worldly interest of the public at large. This kind of professional power exists only in societies in which élite membership itself is legitimized or acquired by professional status. △ [Professional power is a specialized form of the privilege to prescribe. It is this power of prescription that gives control within the industrial state.] The profession's power over the work its members do is therefore distinct and new both in scope and in origin.

Merchants sell you the goods they stock. Guildsmen guarantee quality. Some craftspeople tailor their product to your measure or fancy. Professionals tell you what you need and claim the power to prescribe. They not only recommend what is good, but actually ordain what is right. Neither income, long training, delicate tasks nor social standing is the mark of the professional. Rather, [it is his authority to define a person as client, to determine that person's need and to hand the person a prescription.] This professional authority comprises three roles: the sapiential authority to advise, instruct and direct; the moral authority that makes its acceptance not just useful but obligatory; and charismatic authority that allows the professional to appeal to some supreme interest of his client that not only outranks conscience but sometimes even the *raison d'état.* For instance, the *physician* became the *doctor* when he left commerce in drugs to the pharmacist and kept prescription for himself. He became a *health scientist* when his cartel integrated these authorities in himself and began to deal with cases rather than with persons; he thus protects society's rather than the patient's interests. The authorities that, during the liberal age, had coalesced in the individual practitioner in his treatment of a client are now appropriated by the professional corporation. This entity carves out for itself a social mission. It is a fact that only during the last twenty-five years medicine has turned from a liberal into a dominant profession by obtaining this power to dictate what constitutes a health need for *people in general.* Health specialists as a corporation have acquired the authority to determine what health care must be provided to society. It is no longer the individual professional who imputes a "need" to the individual client, but a corporate agency that imputes to entire classes of people their needs, and claims the mandate to test the whole population in order to identify all those who belong to the group of potential patients.

The difference between craftsman, liberal professional and the new technocrat can be clarified by emphasizing the typical reaction towards people who neglect to take their respective advice. By not taking the craftsman's counsel, you were a fool.

For not taking liberal counsel, you were a masochist. Now the heavy arm of the law may reach out when you escape from the care that your surgeon or shrink have decided for you.

From merchant-craftsman or learned adviser, the professional has mutated into a crusading and commandeering philanthropist. He knows how infants must be fed, which student is or is not to go for higher education, and what drugs people may or may not ingest. From a tutor who guided and watched over you while you memorized your lesson, the schoolmaster has mutated into an educator whose legal status entitles him to a moralizing crusade in which he pushes himself between you and anything you want to learn. Even the dog-catchers of Chicago have mutated into authoritative experts on canine control.

Professionals assert secret knowledge about human nature, knowledge which only they have the right to dispense. They claim a monopoly over the definition of deviance and the remedies needed. For example, lawyers hold that they alone have the competence, and the *legal* right to provide assistance in divorce. Gravediggers become members of a profession by calling themselves morticians, by obtaining college credentials, or by increasing the standing of their trade by electing one of themselves president of the Lion's Club. Morticians form a *profession* when they acquire the muscle to have the police stop your burial if you are not embalmed and boxed by them. In any area where a human need can be imagined these new professions, dominant, authoritative, monopolistic, legalized — and, at the same time, debilitating and effectively disabling the individual—have become exclusive experts of the public good.

ESTABLISHED PROFESSIONS

The transformation of a liberal into a dominant profession is akin to the legal establishment of a state church. Physicians transmogrified into biocrats, teachers into gnosocrats, morticians into thanatocrats are much closer to state supported clergies than to trade associations. The professional as teacher of the currently accepted brand of scientific orthodoxy acts as theologian. As moral entrepreneur and as creator of the need for his services, he acts the role of priest. As crusading helper, he acts the part of the missioner and hunts down the underprivileged. As inquisitor, he outlaws the unorthodox: he imposes his solutions on the recalcitrant who refuses to recognize that he is a problem. This multifaceted investiture with the task of relieving a specific inconvenience of man's estate turns each profession into the analogue of an established cult.

The public acceptance of domineering professions is essentially a political event. Each new establishment of professional legitimacy means that the political tasks of law-making, judicial review and executive power lose some of their proper character and independence. Public affairs pass from the layperson's elected peers into the hands of a self-accrediting élite. When medicine recently outgrew its liberal restraints, it invaded legislation by establishing public norms. Physicians had always determined what constitutes disease; dominant

20

medicine now determines what diseases society shall not tolerate. Medicine invaded the courts. Physicians had always diagnosed who is sick; dominant medicine, however, brands those who must be treated. Liberal practitioners prescribed a cure: dominant medicine has public power of correction; it decides what shall be done with or to the sick. In a democracy, the power to make laws, execute them and achieve public justice must derive from the citizens themselves. But the professionals have taken over citizen control over key powers now restricted, weakened and sometimes abolished by the rise of these church-like professions. Government by a congress that bases its decisions on expert opinions given by professions might be government for, but never by the people. This is not the place to investigate the intent with which political rule was thus weakened; it is sufficient to indicate this subversion and to pinpoint its effects.

Citizen liberties are grounded on the rule that hearsay is excluded from testimony on which public decisions are based. What people can see for themselves and interpret themselves is the common ground for binding rules. Opinions, beliefs, inferences or persuasions must not stand when in conflict with the eyewitness—ever. Expert élites became dominant professions only by reversing this rule. In the legislature and in the courts, the rule against hearsay evidence was suspended in favour of opinions profferred by members of self-accredited élites.

But let us not confuse the public use of expert factual knowledge with a profession's corporate exercise of normative judgement. When a craftsman, such as a gunmaker, was called into court as an expert to reveal to the jury the secrets of his trade, he apprenticed on the spot the jury to his craft. He demonstrated visibly his limited and circumscribed expertise and enabled the jury to decide for themselves from which barrel the bullet might have come. Today, most experts play a different role. The dominant professional provides jury or legislature with his own and fellow-initiates' global opinion, rather than with factual self-limiting evidence and specific skill. Armed with an aura of divine authority, he calls for a suspension of the hearsay rule and inevitably undermines the rule of law. Thus, one sees how democratic power is subverted by an unquestioned assumption of an all-embracing professionalism.

IMPUTABLE NEEDS

Professions could not become dominant and disabling unless people were already experiencing as a lack that which the expert imputes to them as a need. When I learned to speak, *problems* existed only in mathematics or chess; *solutions* were saline or legal, and *need* was mainly used as a verb. The expressions, "I have a problem", or, "I have a need", both sounded silly. As I grew into my teens, and Hitler worked at solutions, the "social problem" also spread. "Problem" children of ever newer shades were discovered among the poor as social workers learned to brand their prey and to standardize their "needs". Need, used as a noun, became the fodder on which professions were

22

fattened into dominance. Poverty was modernized. The poor became the "needy".

During the second half of my life, to be "needy" became respectable. Computable and imputable needs moved up the social ladder. It ceased to be a sign of poverty to have needs. Increased income opened new registers of need. Spock, Comfort and vulgarizers of Nader trained laymen to shop for solutions to problems that had been cooked up according to professional recipes. Schooling qualified graduates to climb ever more rarefied heights and implant and cultivate ever newer strains of hybridized needs. Prescribed packages defined welfare and personal competence shrank. For example, in medicine, ever more "ills" become "illnesses" to be treated by doctors and people lost their will and ability to cope with indisposition, or even with discomfort. Now welfare equals prescribed remedies. In US supermarkets, about 1500 new products appear each year; more than 80% prove useless and unmarketable within a year. Increasingly, consumers are forced to seek guidance from professional consumer protectors to make their choice for them.

Further, the rapid turnover of products renders wants shallow and plastic. Paradoxically, then, high aggregate consumption resulting from engineered needs fosters growing consumer indifference to *specific,* potentially felt wants. Increasingly, needs are created by the advertising slogan, purchases made by prescription. One's action is not the result of personal experience in satisfaction, and the ensuing adaptive consumer substitutes learned for felt needs. As people become experts in the art of learning to need, learning to identify wants from experience becomes a rare competence. As needs are broken down into ever smaller component parts, each managed by the appropriate specialist, the consumer experiences difficulty in integrating the separate offerings of his various tutors into a meaningful whole that could be desired with commitment and possessed with pleasure. The income managers, lifestyle counsellors, food fadist experts, sensitivity developers and others of this ilk clearly perceive the new possibilities for management, and move in to match commodities to the splintered needs and fractured self-confidence of the users.

Used as a noun, "need" is the individual offprint of a professional pattern; it is a plastic-foam replica of the cast with which professionals coin their staple; it is the advertized shape of the honeycomb out of which consumers are made. To be ignorant or unconvinced of one's own needs has become the unforgivable anti-social act. The good citizen is he who imputes stapled needs to himself with such conviction that he drowns out any desire for alternatives, much less the renunciation of need.

When I was born, before Stalin, Hitler and Roosevelt came to power, only the rich, hypochondriacs and members of élite groups spoke of their need for medical care when their temperature rose. It was a questionable and questioned need, since doctors could not do much more than great-grandmothers had done. The first mutation of needs came with sulfa and antibiotics. As the control of infections became a simple and effective routine, drugs went more and more on prescription. Assignment of the sick-role became a medical monopoly. The person who felt *ill* had to go to the clinic to be labelled with a *disease*-name and be legitimately declared a member of the minority of the so-called sick: people were excused from work, entitled to help, put under doctor's orders and enjoined to heal to become useful again. The second mutation of medical needs happened when the sick ceased to be a minority. By the late sixties one out of every two citizens in most western countries were active cases simultaneously in more than three therapeutic agencies. Each one's teeth, womb, blood pressure, psyche, or work-habits were observed, diagnosed, corrected. Multiple patient-relationship became a sign of desirable rather than deplorable health. To be an active client of several professionals provides you now with a well-defined place within the realm of service-consumers for the sake of whom our society functions. Under professional dominance the economy is organized for deviant majorities and their keepers.

At this critical moment, imputed needs move into a third mutation. They coalesce into what the experts call a "multidisciplinary problem" necessitating, therefore, a multiprofessional solution. First, the multiplication of commodities, each tending to turn into a requirement for modernized man, effectively trained the consumer to need on command. Next, the progressive fragmentation of needs into ever smaller and unconnected parts made the client dependent on professional judgement for the blending of his needs into a meaningful whole. The automobile industry provides a useful, though devious, example. By the end of the sixties, the advertised optional equipment making a basic Ford desirable had been multiplied immensely. But contrary to the customer's expectations, this "optional" flim-flam is in fact installed on the assembly line of the Detroit factory and the shopper in Plains is left with a choice between a few packaged samples that are shipped at random: he can either buy a convertible that he wanted but with the green seats he hates, or he can humour his girl-friend with leopard skin seats—at the cost of buying a paisley hard-top.

Finally, the client is trained to need a team-approach to receive what his guardians consider "satisfaction". Personal services which improve the consumer illustrate the point. Therapeutic affluence has exhausted the available life-time of those whom service-professionals diagnose as standing in need of even more services. The intensity of the service-economy has made the time needed for the consumption of pedagogical, medical and social treatments increasingly scarce. Time scarcity may soon turn into the major obstacle for the consumption of prescribed, and often publicly-financed, services. Signs of such scarcity become evident from one's early years. Already in kindergarten, the child is subjected to management by a team made up of such specialists as the allergist, speech pathologist, pediatrician, child psychologist, social worker, physical education instructor and teacher. By forming such a pedocratic team, many different professionals attempt to share the time which has become the major limiting factor in the imputation of further needs. For the adult, it is not the school, but the work-place where the packaging of services focusses. The personnel manager, labour educator, in-service trainer, insurance planner, consciousness-raiser find it more profitable to share the worker's time, rather than compete for it. A need-less citizen would be highly suspicious. People are told that they need their jobs, not so much for the money as for the services they get. The commons are extinguished and replaced by a new placenta built of funnels that deliver professional service. Life is paralyzed in permanent intensive care.

FIVE ILLUSIONS

The disabling of the citizen through professional dominance is completed through the power of illusion. Religion finally becomes displaced, not by the state or the waning of the faith, but by professional establishments and client confidence. The professionals appropriate the special knowledge to define public issues in terms of problems. The acceptance of this claim legitimizes the docile recognition of imputed lacks on the part of the layman: his world turns into an echo-chamber of needs. This dominance is reflected in the skyline of the city. Professional buildings look down on the crowds that shuttle between them in a continual pilgrimage to the new cathedrals of insurance, health, education and welfare. Homes are transformed into hygienic apartments where one cannot be born, cannot be sick and cannot die decently. Not only are helpful neighbours a vanishing species, but so are liberal doctors who make housecalls. Work places fit for apprenticeship turn into opaque mazes of corridors that permit access only to functionaries equipped with "identities". Professional environments are the last refuge for addicts to remedies.

The prevailing addiction to imputable needs on the part of the rich, and the paralyzing fascination with needs on the part of the poor would indeed be irreversible if people actually fitted the calculus of needs. But this is not so. Beyond a certain level, medicine engenders helplessness and disease; education turns into the major generator of a disabling division of labour; fast transportation systems turn urbanized people for 17% of their waking hours into passengers, and for an equal amount of time into members of the road gang that works to pay Ford, Esso and the highway department. Social services create helplessness and legal agencies injustice.

Our major institutions have acquired the uncanny power to subvert the very purposes for which they had been engineered and financed originally. Under the rule of our most prestigious professions, our institutional tools have as their principal product paradoxical counterproductivity—the systematic disabling of the citizenry. A city built around wheels becomes inappropriate for feet.

Why are there no rebellions against the drift into disabling service delivery systems? The chief explanation must be sought in the illusion-generating power that these same systems possess. Besides doing technical things to body and mind, professionalism also is a powerful ritual which generates credence in the thing it does. Besides teaching Johnny to read, schools also teach him that learning from teachers is better. Besides providing locomotion, prestige, sexual licence and a sense of power packaged together, the automobile puts walking out of step. Besides providing help in seeking legal remedies, lawyers also convey the notion that they solve personal problems. Besides printing the news, papers also teach by their stories that doctors are curing cancer. An ever growing part of our major institutions' functions is the cultivation and maintenance of five illusions which turn the citizen into a client to be saved by experts.

The Discounting of Use-Value

The first enslaving illusion is the idea that people are born to be consumers and that they can attain any of their goals by purchasing goods and services. This illusion is due to an educated blindness for the worth of use-values in the total economy. In none of the economic models serving as national guidelines is there a variable to account for non-marketable use-values any more than there is a variable for nature's perennial contribution. Yet, there is no economy that would not collapse immediately if use-value production contracted beyond a point through, for example, home-making done for wages, or marital sex only at a fee. What people do or make but will not or cannot put up for sale is as immeasurable and as invaluable for the economy as the oxygen they breathe.

The illusion that economic models can ignore use-values springs from the assumption that those activities that we designate by intransitive verbs can be indefinitely substituted with institutionally-defined staples referred to by nouns. Education replaces "I learn"; health care replaces "I heal"; transportation replaces "I move"; TV replaces "I play".

The confusion of personal and stapled values has

spread through most domains. Under professional leadership, use-values are dissolved, rendered obsolete and finally deprived of their distinct nature. Ten years of running a farm can be thrown into a pedagogical mixer and be made equivalent to a high school certificate. Things picked up at random and hatched in the freedom of the street are added as "educational experience" to things funnelled into pupils heads. The knowledge accountants seem unaware that curriculum and experience, like oil and water, mix only as long as they are osterized by educational research. Gangs of crusading need-catchers could not continue to tax us, nor could they spend our resources on their tests, networks and other nostrums unless we are and remain paralyzed by our greedy beliefs.

The usefulness of staples, or packaged commodities, is intrinsically limited by two boundaries that must not be confused. First, queues will sooner or later stop the operation of any system that produces needs faster than the corresponding commodity, and second, dependence on commodities will sooner or later so determine needs, that the autonomous production of a functional analogue will be paralyzed. *Congestion* and *paralysis* are both results of escalation in any sector of production, albeit results of a very different kind. Congestion, which is a measure of the degree to which staples get into their own way, explains why mass transportation by private car in Manhattan would be useless; it does not explain why people work hard to buy and insure cars they cannot profitably use. Even less does congestion alone explain why people become so dependent on vehicles that they are paralyzed, and just cannot take to their feet.

People become prisoners to time-consuming acceleration, stupefying education and sick-making medicine because beyond a certain threshold of intensity dependence on a bill of industrial and professional goods destroys human potential, and does so in a specific way. Only up to a point can commodities replace what people make or do on their own. Only within limits can exchange-values satisfactorily replace use-values. Beyond this point, further production serves the interests of the professional producer—who has imputed the need to the consumer—and leaves the consumer befuddled and giddy, albeit more affluent. Needs satisfied rather than merely fed must be determined to a significant degree by the pleasure that is derived from personal autonomous action. There are boundaries beyond which commodities cannot be multiplied without disabling their consumer for this self-affirmation in action.

Humans, as distinguished from apes, make and use tools. Mankind is partitioned not into strains or races but into cultures, each distinguished by its set of tools. Traditionally, these tools are labour-intensive: most needs that people perceive at any time are determined by their acquaintance with a tool by which they can produce that which will satisfy their need. Man ceases to be one of his own kind when he can no longer shape his own needs by the more or less competent tools that his culture provides. Women or men, who have come to depend almost entirely on deliveries of standardized fragments produced by tools that are operated by

31

anonymous others, cease to live human lives, and at best barely survive — even though they do so surrounded by glitter. Ultimately, they lose even the ability to discriminate between living and survival. Valued experience, free movement, dwelling arrangements, the sense of security and participation in community affairs each springs from two distinct sources: personal aliveness and engineered provisions. Packages alone inevitably frustrate the consumer when their delivery paralyzes him. The measure of well-being in a society is thus never like an equation by which these two modes of production are added; it is always like a balance that results when use-values and commodities fruitfully mesh in synergy. Only up to a point can heteronomous production of commodities enhance and complement the autonomous production of the corresponding personal purpose. Beyond this point, the synergy between the two modes of production, i.e. self-guided and other-directed, paradoxically turns against the purpose for which both use-value and commodity were intended.

The fundamental reason for counterproductivity must be sought in the specific environmental impact that results from every form of mass production. Medicine makes culture unhealthy; education tends to obscure the environment; vehicles wedge highways between the points they ought to bridge. Each of these institutions, beyond a critical point of its growth, thus exercises a radical monopoly.

A commercial monopoly merely corners the market for one brand of penicillin, whisky or car. An industry-wide cartel corners all mass transportation in favour of tyres. A radical monopoly goes further: it deprives the environment of those features that people need in a specific area to subsist outside the market economy. An industry-wide cartel favours one industrial technology over another. A radical monopoly paralyzes autonomous action in favour of professional deliveries. The more completely vehicles dislocate people, the more traffic managers will be needed, and the more powerless people will be to walk home. This radical monopoly would accompany high-speed traffic even if motors were powered by sunshine and vehicles were spun of air. The longer each person is in the grip of education, the less time and inclination he has for browsing and surprise. At some point in every domain, the amount of goods delivered so degrade the environment for action that the possible synergy between use-values and commodities turns negative. Paradoxical counterproductivity sets in.

TECHNOLOGICAL PROGRESS

The second enslaving illusion conceptualizes technological progress as a kind of engineering product licencing more professional domination. This delusion says that tools, in order to become more efficient in the pursuit of a specific purpose, inevitably become more complex and inscrutable. Therefore, they necessarily require special operators who are highly trained and who alone can be securely trusted. Actually, just the opposite is true, and ought to occur. As techniques multiply and become more specific, their use often requires less complex judgements and skills. They no longer require that trust on the part of the client on which

33

the autonomy of the liberal professional, and even that of the craftsman, was built. From a social point of view, we ought to reserve the designation "technical progress" to instances in which new tools expand the capacity and the effectiveness of a wider range of people, especially when new tools permit more autonomous production of use-values.

There is nothing *inevitable* about the expanding professional monopoly over new technology. The great inventions of the last hundred years, such as new metals, ball-bearings, some building materials, circuitry, some tests and remedies, are capable of increasing both the power of the autonomous and of the heteronomous modes of production. There is no simple "technological imperative". In fact, however, most new technology is not being incorporated into convivial equipment, but into institutional packages and complexes. The professionals rather consistently use industrial production to establish a radical monopoly by means of technology's clear effectiveness. Counterproductivity due to the paralysis of use-value production is fostered by this notion of technological progress.

JEANS, BUT ONLY FROM CARDIN

The third disabling myth expects that effective tools for lay-use must first be certified by professional tests. The people who take this stance see that counterproductivity cannot be stopped except by redressing the balance between heteronomous-industrial and autonomous-community production. They also understand that community assessment must replace the current expert assessment of equipment and products. But many proponents of soft technology stay hooked on professional service because they assume that appropriate technology in the hands of the layman will compete with industry only when present tools have been redesigned for the man in the street. They wait for the ultimate bicycle, the supreme windmill, the safe pill, the perfect solar panel. Such people remain entranced by the professional dream that good things will be forever replaced by better things. They are snobs for whom the tool with which everyman will beat the multinationals must of necessity come out of research and design rituals as solemn as those that synthesize the alleged miracles at Dupont and LaRoche.

THE SCRAMBLING OF LIBERTIES AND RIGHTS

The fourth disabling illusion looks to experts for limits to growth. Entire populations socialized to need what they are told they need will now be told what they do *not* need. The same multinational agents that for a generation imposed an international standard on bookkeeping, deodorants and energy consumption on rich and poor alike, now sponsor the Club of Rome. Obediently, UNESCO gets into the act and trains experts in the regionalization of imputed needs. For their own imputed good, the rich are thus programmed to pay for more costly professional dominance at home and provide the poor with imputed needs of a cheaper and tighter brand. The brightest of the new professionals clearly see that growing scarcity pushes controls over needs ever upward. The central planning of output-optimal decentralization has become the most prestigious job of 1977. But what is not yet recognized is that this new illusionary salvation by professionally decreed limits confuses liberties and rights.

In each of seven UN-defined world regions a new clergy is trained to preach the appropriate style of austerity drafted by the new need-designers. Consciousness-raisers roam through local communities inciting people to meet the decentralized production goals that have been assigned to them. Milking the family goat was a liberty until more ruthless planning made it a duty to contribute the milk yield to the GNP.

The synergy between autonomous and heteronomous production is reflected in society's balance of liberties versus rights. Liberties protect use-values as rights protect the access to commodities. And just as commodities can extinguish the possibility of producing use-values, and turn into impoverishing wealth, so the professional definition of rights can extinguish liberties and establish a tyranny that smothers people underneath their rights.

CERTIFIED SELF-HELPERS

The fifth enslaving illusion is this year's radical chic. As the prophets of the sixties drooled about development on the doorsteps of affluence these myth makers mouth about the self-help of professionalized clients.

I have seen ads of bathroom cabinets that open their locks only to a duly certified self-medicator. In the U.S. alone, about 2700 books have appeared since 1965 that teach you how to be your own patient, so you only need see the doctor when it is worthwhile for him. Some books recommend that after due training and examination graduates in self-medication should be empowered to buy aspirin and dispense it to their children. Others suggest that professionalized patients shall receive preferential rates in hospitals and that they should benefit from lower insurance premiums. Only women with a licence to practice home birth should have their children outside hospitals since such professional mothers can, if needed, be sued by themselves for malpractice on themselves. I have seen a "radical" proposal that such a license to give birth could be obtained under feminist rather than medical auspices.

The professional dream of rooting each hierarchy of needs in the grassroots goes under the banner of self-help. At present it is promoted by the new tribe of experts in self-help who have replaced the international development experts of the sixties. The professionalization of laymen is their aim. U.S. experts in building who last autumn invaded Mexico serve as an example for the new crusade. About two years ago, an M.I.T. professor of architecture came to Mexico for a vacation. A Mexican friend of mine took him beyond the Airport where, during the last twelve years, a new city had grown up. From a few huts, it mushroomed into a community three times the size of Cambridge. My friend, also an architect, wanted to show the thousands of examples of peasant ingenuity with patterns, structures and uses of refuse not in and therefore not derivable from textbooks. He should not have been surprised that his colleague took several hundred rolls of pictures of these brilliant inventions that make this two-million-person slum work. The pictures were analyzed in Cambridge; and by the end of the year, new-baked U.S. specialists in community architecture were busy teaching the people of Ciudad Netzahualcoyotl their problems, needs and solutions.

THE POST-PROFESSIONAL ETHOS

Some already live, and others are capable of moving, beyond the Age of Disabling Professions and its glittering shopping centres for goods and services. The days of politicians who promise more inclusive packages of welfare are numbered; soon, they will receive the same reception formerly accorded priest-ridden electoral slates and the verbiage of Marxist epigones. Professional cartels are now as brittle as the French clergy in the age of Voltaire; soon, the still inchoate post-professional ethos will reveal the iron cage of their nakedness. The professional peddlers of health, education, welfare and peace of mind required almost twenty-five years to establish their control over who *ought* to get what and why. For a long time, yet, they might also be able to control who *shall* get what, and at what cost, acting like gangsters. But unbeknownst to them, their credibility fades fast. A post-professional ethos takes shape in the spirit of those who begin to see the emperor's true physiognomy.

Thousands of individuals and groups now

challenge professional dominance over themselves and the socio-technical conditions in which they live. They do so by the questions they ask and the style of life which they consciously create. In the social wasteland that sprawls between the union-ized dullness of Middle America and the smug spirituality of orthodox protest, I continually bump into these people and tribes. True, they are still a disparate lot, only seeing through the smog, darkly. But they begin to recognize what they must abandon to live. Further, groups continue to amaze themselves because of their tolerance for the quite different style in which the tribe squatting on the next plot chooses to live.

These non-ideological minorities may turn into a political force. The age of Disabling Professions may very well close when these silent minorities can clarify the philosophical and legal character of what in common *they do not want.* The advantages of self-chosen joyful austerity evidenced by these people will acquire political form and weight only when combined with a general theory that places freedom within publicly chosen limits above claims for ever more costly packages of "rights".But the post-professional society cannot be summed up, nor, by its very essence, can its design characteristics be predicted or predicated. We are incapable of imagining what free men can do when equipped with modern tools respectfully constrained. The Post-Professional Ethos will hopefully result in a social panorama more colourful and diverse than all the cultures of past and present taken together.

IRVING KENNETH ZOLA

Healthism and Disabling Medicalization

My theme is that medicine is becoming a major institution of social control incorporating the more traditional institutions of religion and law. It is becoming the new repository of truth, the place where absolute and often final judgements are made by supposedly morally neutral and objective experts. And these judgements are no longer made in the name of virtue or legitimacy but in the name of health. Moreover this is not occurring through any increase in the political power of physicians. It is instead an insidious and often undramatic phenomenon, accomplished by 'medicalizing' much of daily living, by making medicine and the labels "healthy" and "ill" *relevant* to an ever increasing part of human existence.

A SPECULATIVE HISTORY

Concern with medical influence is not new. Over a hundred years ago Goethe feared that the modern world might turn into one giant medical institution. Philip Rieff updated this concern when he noted that 'the hospital is succeeding the church and the parliament as the archetypal institution of Western culture.'[1] This shift, one that is far from complete has spanned centuries. To understand this phenomenon we must be aware of two rather important characteristics of professions. Their control of their work and their tendency to generalize their expertise beyond technical matters. Everett Hughes stated these characteristics rather concisely:

> Not merely do the practitioners, by by virtue of gaining admission to the charmed circle of colleagues, individually exercise the license to do things others do not, but collectively they presume to tell society what is good and right for the individual and for society at large in some aspect of life. Indeed, they set the very terms in which people may think about this aspect of life.[2]

[1] Philip Rieff, *Freud: The Mind of the Moralist,* Garden City: Doubleday, 1961, p.340.

[2] Cited in Eliot Freidson, *Profession of Medicine,* New York: Dodd, Mead & Co., 1970, p.204.

42

How a professional gains the exclusive right and licence to manage its work has been documented very well by others.[1] For now I wish to dwell on the second aspect—what Bittner has stated as a profession's desire to extend its limits beyond its technically and traditionally ascribed and assumed competence to wider more diffuse spheres.[2] It is here that we enter our brief examination of religion, law and medicine.

The Christian ministry as the prototype of all professions is as good a place as any to start. Ever since Christianity achieved its European dominance in the early Middle Ages, its ministry wrestled with the conflicts between its limited and diffuse functions. The former involved the specific administration of the means of grace to individuals, while the latter involved the functions of prophecy—the direct application of the message of the gospel to the structure of the community. It is in the conveyance and elaboration of "this message" that the Christian ministry wove itself deeply into communal life. Thus, well into the Reformation one could claim that all communities were in a real sense religious ones, all leaders religiously committed, and the meaning and values of all relationships derived from a religious framework.

But during the seventeenth and eighteenth centuries the influence of religious teachings on

---

[1] Freidson *op. cit.,* is the best source.

[2] Much of the following historical perspective is derived from Egon Bittner's seminal article "The Structure of Psychiatric Influence", *Mental Hygiene,* Vol. 52, July 1968, pp. 423-430. The original thoughts are his, the distortions are mine.

community life faded. In England, some date this to the 1640's, the Age of Cromwell, when the common law was becoming the law of the land. Though it is perhaps impossible to pinpoint a single cause, the culmination may be seen in what Hobsbaum called the dual revolution[1] — the Industrial Revolution itself, not a single event but one spanning literally centuries as well as the French Revolution and its concomitants. As the Industrial Revolution drastically altered the relationship within and between communities, families and people, a new basis to explain as well as define (and perhaps to control) these relationships was sought. The old order faded and a new codifier was needed. The seeding had been going on for a long time. Tracts were being written about the nature of man based on a less transcendental framework. They embodied the concept of the social contract. Their terms were legalistic and their espousers, Hobbes, Rousseau, Mills, Locke, were of varying persuasion. The American and French Constitutions perhaps enthroned the tools and transformation of this thinking. They spoke of human affairs without religious reference but rather in secular terms such as justice, right, duty, franchise, liberty, contract. And as once it had been in religious teaching, so now the search for the meaning and understanding of human life was sought in the law. In America it was a sentiment well expressed in the coloquialism 'there ought to be a law'. And this law was a more earthly task-master. Where once we sought truth in

[1] E.J. Hobsbaum, *The Age of Revolution—Europe 1789-1848*, London: Weidenfeld and Nicolson, 1962

delineating the wisdom of God, now we sought answers in deciphering the nature of man. And when we found such truth we reified it, at least in rhetoric, saying 'that no man was above the law'.

Religion of course did not fade away but concentrated more on matters of the inner life leaving the secular sphere to law. And flourish it did with little challenge for over a century. But two world wars including "a war to end all wars" led to the questioning of such untoward confidence. And two legal events ironically chimed its death knell—a set of trials in Nuremburg and Jerusalem where men as their defence against charges of genocide evoked without success their obedience to law and authority. In addition, in the United States at least, despite the laws, the poor still seemed poorer, the minorities still exploited, the consumer cheated, until the idea of law itself began to be questioned. The symbol of justice as blindfold was being replaced by one with its eyes slightly open and with its hand slightly extended. In America, a relatively new concept emerged, one almost "unthinkable" a couple of decades previously, the concept of a "bad law". An old tactic caught fire again—civil disobedience and with it debates arose as to the circumstances under which it was just to violate the law. Again the interpretative system of values was beginning to crumble.

There is another way of stating this historical situation. Bittner has said it most eloquently: 'The utlimate ground of Christian influence, its charisma was *The Truth*. (This does not mean) that what was preached was true or not true but merely that it was with reference to its truth-value that the claims of Christian influence were asserted. In an equally fundamental sense, the idea of *authority* was the basis of the influence of jurisprudence . . . Obviously it cannot be said that Christianity did not claim authority; nor can it be maintained that the law neglected questions of truth. However, what in the former was the authority of truth became in the latter the truth of authority. The crisis of the ministry and of jurisprudence consists precisely in the fact that the former could not sustain its truth claims and that the latter was failing in its authority claims'.[1]

But again there was another group of codifiers waiting in the wings—new purveyors of both truth and authority. Medical Science was there to fill the vacuum.

WHY MEDICAL SCIENCE

First, there is a why of the where—why this phenomenon is reflected in the United States more clearly than elsewhere.

Perhaps it is necessary to state almost a truism, that modern medicine has never succeeded nor been accepted in any country just because it is better in some way than the existing method nor even if it can be shown to significantly reduce mortality or disability.[2] Thus, we can more easily

[1] Bittner, *op. cit.*, p. 427

[2] This is amply demonstrated in the many case studies of western public health programmes introduced into non-western countries. (See Ben Paul, editor, *Health Community and Society*, New York: Russell Sage, 1955).

understand the acceptance of medical science in the United States by noting its fit with at least three central values, which have been dominant almost since the creation of that nation.[1] The first of these can be labelled activism—a continual emphasis on mastering the environment, the struggle of man over nature rather than the effort to adjust or submit to it. In the United States there was no river that could not be dammed, no space that could not be bridged and ultimately no disease that could not be conquered. The idea of conquest is an appropriate one as the United States waged successive "wars" against polio, measles and now against heart disease, stroke, cancer. A second might be called worldliness which consists of a general preference for practical secular pursuits over more aesthetic, mystical, or theoretical ones. This phenomenon was no doubt aided by the absence of any state or institutionalized religion. As a result, medical science had no formidable institutionalized opponent as in other countries. Finally, there is the American valuation on instrumentalism—an emphasis on doing—on doing something, almost anything, when confronted with a problem. "Doing nothing in a difficult situation" was interestingly enough an item diagnostic of neuroticism on a popular American psychological test. Sometimes the emphasis on movement became so great that speed itself was emphasized—sometimes for no logical reason. Where else but in America could a selling

---

[1] Talcott Parsons, 'Definitions of Health and Illness in the Light of American Values on Social Structure' in E.J. Jaco, Ed., *Patients, Physicians and Illness,* Glencoe, Illinois, Free Press, 1972, 2nd Ed., pp. 107-127.

point of a TV-set be that it goes on 30 seconds faster than its nearest competitor.

The second 'why' is the "why of when"—when medical science took hold. Again there is no single event.

With the bacteriological revolution and the Flexner report in the United States, medicine wedded itself not only to science but became the great incorporator of knowledge. Thus, long before it claimed to be the truth, it began to garner to its bosom any form of knowledge (admittedly some more grudgingly than others) that might be relevant to its ends. From biology to physics to economics to psychology to engineering to philosophy to ethics, all found a place in the medical curriculum. And once in, no piece of knowledge seemed ever to be dropped, and so the scope of medical training continued to expand and lengthen. While this apparently may be the source of much consternation to curriculum committees, it did give medicine the claim of being involved in more aspects of life than any other discipline or institution and place it in a central position to be a codifier of the meaning of life in the twentieth century.

Medicine also wedded itself to an important "geist" of the times—the new wave of "humanism". For while medicine was still concerned with the more traditional issues of authority and truth, it brought to preeminence something else—the notion of service, the idea of helping others directly.[1]

[1] Bittner, *op. cit.*, makes this argument in particular for the rise of psychiatry. I would claim its extention to medicine in general.

Other events were happening on the social level—the standard of living, eating, and housing were on the rise and as a result mortality due to all causes in the decline.[1] At very least this gave medicine another kind of relevance vis-à-vis religion. It may seem reaching, but it does not strike me as inconsistent, that religion and notions of the hereafter are especially relevant when "the here" is so lousy and so short. But when "the here" increases dramatically—when more people live to 50, 60 or 70 and suffer from diseases they never dreamed of, such as cancer, heart disease and stroke, then this life and its most concrete embodiment, the human body, becomes of greater interest and concern.

Now we must turn to the final "why"—a more broader ideological fit between the promises of modern medicine and the needs of certain segments of modern society. Again the long-view is necessary.

It is probably safe to say that the wave of legalism introduced by the American and French constitutions brought with it some settling as well as unsettling notions. For in addition to other ways of defining man's life, its meaning, his relationship to others, it used some rather heady concepts like individual liberty, freedom and, perhaps most difficult to take, equality. The words sounded good but "surely" it was not meant to be practised. "Surely" some people were "more equal" than others. So theories and writing began to appear in many fields trying to explain some of the "given" inequalities of man. Amongst the more popular—all done up in the wrappings of scientific measurements

[1] A phenomenon essentially unrelated to medicine—see Dubos, *The Mirage of Health*, Garden City, N.J.: Anchor Books 1961.

and figures, was the phrenology movement and then a text which went through several editions, Count de Gobineau's *The Inequality of the Races.* But all were relatively shortlived. One figure, one theory did, however, "make it" not only as an accepted scientific work, but as a guide for social action—a theory which in relatively short time reached what Bertrand Russell called the "cult of common usage". This was the concept of evolution, the work of Charles Darwin. It had an enormous appeal. For though the idea of evolution was not new, the process by which he postulated it taking place was: a competition, the survival of the fittest. What was applicable to flora and fauna was seen also to be relevant for man. For whatever else it implied, it seemed to be an easy step to say that what is here today is here because it is in some way better. This was applied not only to civilizations but ultimately to man vis-à-vis other men, the people who at this point in time were on top were there because in some way they deserved to be. Though we often tend to think of Darwin's theory as anti-religion or even anti-the established society, it is apparent that some people did see the forest for the trees. Upon hearing the postulates at a scientific congress, one attender is reported to have said, 'Sir, you are preaching scientific Calvinism with biological determinism replacing religious predestination'.

Instead of a fixity of the universe, of hierarchical relations promulgated by God, we now had a universe fixed by scientific laws. As judged by the political, social, and legal implementations of such theorizing, many more people seemed willing to act upon this thinking though they might not acknowledge it directly. Thus, it would be my contention that much of science and later medical science in its notion of progress had a particular kind of progress at least latently in mind. Medical science became the ultimate articulator and conveyor of the message of Darwin and Spencer. This was a social message more comforting to an understanding of social order than say some of the other competing views like those of Saint-Simon, Marx and Engels and a more comforting social approach than the abortive revolutions of 1848. So, too, medical science began to define progress as well as the meaning of life in new terms. Health itself became not merely the means to some larger end but the end in itself, no longer one of the essential pillars of the good life but the very definition of what is the good life. Its full articulation was seen in the 1948 World Health Organization declaration that health was 'a state of complete physical, mental, and social being and not merely the absence of disease and infirmity'. Its codifiers carried not the Bible or Blackstone but the Merck Manual. Robes remained but changed in colour from red and black to white.

THE MEDICALIZING OF SOCIETY

The burgeoning influence of medicine is, as I said, more insidious and undramatic than the forces of religion and law. Its full exercise awaited the twentieth century. Only now is the process of 'medicalization' upon us—a phenomenon which Freidson has operationalized most succinctly:

> The medical profession has first claim to jurisdiction over the label of illness and *anything* to which it may be attached, irrespective of its capacity to deal with it effectively.[1]

For illustrative purposes this 'attaching' process may be categorized in four concrete ways:

1. Through the expansion of what in life is deemed relevant to the good practice of medicine.
2. Through the retention of absolute control over certain technical procedures.
3. Through the retention of near absolute access to certain "taboo" areas.
4. Through the expansion of what in medicine is deemed relevant to the good practice of life.

1. The expansion of what in life is deemed relevant to the good practice of medicine

The gradual change of medicine's commitment from a specific etiological model of disease to a multi-casual one as well as its increasing acceptance of such concepts as comprehensive medicine and psychosomatics has enormously expanded that which is or can be relevant to the understanding, treatment and even prevention of disease. Thus, it is no longer merely necessary for the patient to divulge the symptoms of his body but also the symptoms of daily living, his habits and his worries. Part of this is greatly facilitated in the "age of the computer". For what might be too embarrassing, or take too long, or be inefficient in a face-to-face

[1] Eliot Freidson, *Profession of Medicine, op. cit.,* p. 251.

encounter can now be asked and analyzed impersonally by the machine, and moreover be done before the patient ever sees the physician. With the advent of the computer a certain guarantee of privacy is necessarily lost, for while many physicians might have probed similar issues, the only place the data was stored was in the mind of the doctor and only rarely in the medical record. The computer, on the other hand, has a retrievable, transmittable and almost inexhaustible memory.

It is not merely, however, the nature of the data needed to make more "accurate" diagnoses and treatments but the perspective which accompanies it—a perspective which pushes the physician far beyond his office and the exercise of technical skills. To rehabilitate or at least alleviate many of the ravages of chronic disease, it has become increasingly necessary to intervene to change permanently the habits of a patient's lifetime—be it of working, sleeping, playing, and eating. In Prevention, the "extension into life" goes even deeper. Since the very idea of primary prevention means getting there *before* the disease process starts, the physician must not only seek out his clientèle but once found must often convince them that they must do something *now* and perhaps at a time when the potential patient feels well or not especially troubled. The recent findings of genetics push this perspective even further. For individuals are now being confronted with making decisions, not about diseases which may occur in their own life span, but in those of their children or grandchildren.

2. Through the retention of absolute control over certain technical procedures

In particular this refers to skills which in certain jurisdictions are the very operational and legal definition of the practice of medicine—the right to do surgery and prescribe drugs. Both of these take medicine far beyond concern with ordinary organic diseases.

In surgery this is seen in several different sub-specialties. The plastic surgeon has at least participated in, if not helped perpetuate, certain aesthetic standards. What once was a practice confined to restoration has now expanded beyond the correction of certain traumatic or even congenital deformities to the creation of new physical properties from the shape of one's nose to the size of one's breast. Again and again it seems as if medicine is trying to prove Ortega Y Gassett's statement that man has no nature, only a history. Thus, many of the accompaniments of formerly considered "natural processes" come under medical purview—as in ageing. Now failing sight, hearing, teeth become of greater medical concern and chemical and surgical interventions to deal with wrinkles, sagging and hair loss become more common. Alterations in sexual and reproductive functioning have long been a medical concern. Yet today the frequency of hysterectomies seems not so highly correlated with the presence of organic disease, and what avenues the very possibility of sex change will open is anyone's guess. Though here too we are reminded of medicine's responsibility.

The surgical treatment of the conditions

of hermaphroidism and pseudohermaphroidism to correct nature's mistakes, that the sexual identity and function of such persons may be established, has long been accepted as a contribution of medical science to suffering mankind.[1]

Transplantations, despite their still relative infrequency, have had a tremendous effect on our very notions of death and dying. And at the other end of life's continuum, since abortion is still essentially a surgical procedure, it is to the physician-surgeon that society is turning (and the physician-surgeon accepting) for criteria and guidelines as to when life begins.

In the exclusive right to prescribe and thus pronounce on and regulate drugs the power of the physician is even more awesome. Forgetting for the moment our obsession with youth's "illegal" use of drugs, any observer can see, judging by sales alone, that the greatest increase in drug use over the last ten years has not been in the realm of treating any organic disease but in treating a large number of psychosocial states:

To help us sleep or keep us awake.

To stimulate our appetite or decrease it.

To tone down our energy level or to increase it.

To relieve our depression or activate our interests.

To enhance our memory, our intelligence and our vision—spiritually or otherwise.

[1] D.H. Russell, 'The Sex-Conversion Controversy,' *New England Journal of Medicine,* Vol. 279, 1968, p. 535.

A former commissioner of the U.S. Food and Drug Administration went so far as to predict:

> We will see new drugs, more targeted, more specific and more potent than anything we have . . . And many of these would be for people we would call healthy.[1]

3. Through the retention of near absolute access to certain "taboo" areas

These "taboo" areas refer to medicine's almost exclusive licence to examine and treat, that most personal of individual possessions—the inner workings of our bodies and minds. My contention is that if anything can be shown in some way to affect the workings of the body and to a lesser extent the mind, then it can be labelled an 'illness itself, or *jurisdictionally* a medical problem'. The sheer statistical import of this can be seen by looking at only four such problems: ageing, drug addiction, alcoholism, pregnancy. The first and last were once regarded as normal, natural processes and the middle two as human foibles and weaknesses. Now this has changed and to some extent medical specialties have emerged to meet these new needs. Numerically it expands medicine's involvement not only in a longer span of human existence but opens the possibility of its services to millions if not billions of people. In the United States, the implication of declaring alcoholism a disease (the import of a Supreme Court Decision as well as

[1] J.L. Goddard quoted in the *Boston Globe,* August 7, 1966.

laws currently under consideration in several state legislatures) would reduce arrests in many jurisdictions by ten to fifty per-cent and transfer such "offenders" when "discovered" directly to a medical facility. It is pregnancy, however, which produces a most illuminating illustration. For in the United States it was barely 70 years ago when virtually all births and their concomitants occurred outside the hospital as well as outside medical supervision. I do not have a precise documentary history, but with this medical claim solidified so too was medicine's claim to whole hosts of related processes: not only birth but prenatal, postnatal and pediatric care; not only conception but infertility; not only the process of reproduction but the process and problems of sexual activity itself, not only when life begins in the issue of abortion but whether it should be allowed to begin at all as in genetic counselling. The labelling of pregnancy as a disease has had still further implications in the political and social role of women and their right to control their own bodies. What has happened in this arena becomes even of greater concern when we talk about ageing. For while some of us take drugs, and a few more of us drink, and half of us have the possibility of having babies, all of us age. The tone is set by Ilya Metchnikoff, a pioneer in anti-ageing research:

> It is doubtless an error to consider ageing a physiological phenomenon. It can be considered normal because everyone ages, but only to the extent that one might consider normal the pains of childbirth that an anaesthetic might relieve;

> on the contrary, ageing is a *chronic sickness* for which it is much more difficult to find a remedy.[1]

Already this disease model has surfaced in the spectre of heroic measures to save a life at all costs. Will it soon redefine and unwittingly make even worse what it is to be old in a society of youth?

Medicine is also increasing its involvement in another taboo area—what used to be called problems of the soul but now are located in the psyche. A recent British study reported that within a five-year period there had been a notable rise (from 25% to 41%) in the proportion of the population willing to consult the physician with a personal problem.[2] Partly this is through the foothold that medical personnel already hold in "the taboo". For it seems as reported in many studies that access to the body opens up access to other intimate areas as well.[3]

Thus Freidson reports that patients explain their preference for a nurse over a social worker in help with emotional problems because of the former's greater "familiarity" with their situation. One of his cases illustrates this aptly:

> You know, you like to go to someone who knows something about you and I don't know the social worker. I know she took my social history and that we

[1] Ilya Metchnikoff cited in Patrick M. McGrady, Jr., *The Youth Doctors,* New York: Ace, 1969, pp. 283-284.

[2] Karen Dunnel and Ann Cartwright, *Medicine Takers, Prescribers and Hoarders,* London: Routledge and Kegan Paul, 1972.

[3] Irving Kenneth Zola and Sydney Croog, 'Work Perceptions and Their Implications for Professional Identity, *'Social Science and Medicine,* Vol. 2, 1968, pp. 15-28.

always say hello, but I did not know her and I didn't think she really knew much about us and our family. Where the nurse knew about us, she would be the logical one to go to.[1]

The medical profession's growing "popularity" in this area is also due to the simple reduction of other resources. Religion and the clergy have seemed decreasingly "relevant" to the problems of daily living, though there is now a new emphasis on various forms of counselling. Modern living arrangements have also contributed. For whether we look at the suburban spread or the concrete cylinders called "modern urban communities", there seems to be an absence of informal and comfortable places to gather and talk and thus a further reduction in "informal networks of help". Thus, people must of necessity turn to more formal institutions. And they do so in increasing numbers to the only one ready and waiting—medicine.

4. Through the expansion of what in medicine is deemed relevant to the good practice of life

Though in some ways the most powerful of all "the medicalizing of society" processes, the point can be simply made. Here we refer to the role of medicine directly in creating the good life or fending off the bad one.

The most far-reaching social involvement of medicine may well come in the burgeoning field of genetics and its applied arm, genetic counselling.

[1] Eliot Freidson, 'Specialists Without Roots,' *Human Organization,* Vol. 18, Autumn 1959, p. 115.

A 1974 United States government report[1] indicated that the list of recognized genetic disorders now includes nearly 2,000 caused by a single gene and is growing at the rate of 75-100 newly identified disorders each year. Disorders caused by multiple genes or chromosomal defects, such as Down's syndrome (mongolism) are not included, so the number of known disorders is even larger. The list also does not include conditions suspected of a genetic component nor the still largely unknown mutagenic effect of exposure to various environmental factors. From such data it is not especially surprising that a November 1974 article in the Journal of the American Medical Association gave the conservative estimate, based on existing studies of chromosome defects, occurring in one of every two hundred *live* births.[2] In me this provokes the following sociological prediction: Any society that for whatever reason finds itself with a declining birth rate will inevitably be concerned with the quality of those lives that will be produced. And though this inevitably starts with a deselection process whereby we choose *not* to have children with certain genetic defects, the next step is selection to heighten certain characteristics or at least to protect the individual and the society against

[1] Science Policy Research Division, Congressional Research Service, Library of Congress 'Genetic Engineering—Evolution of Technological Issue,' Supplemental Report I prepared for The Subcommittee on Science Research and Development of The Committee on Science and Astronautics, U.S. House of Representatives, Ninety-Third Congress, Washington; U.S. Government Printing Office, December 1974.

[2] Cited in Science Policy Research Division Report *op. cit.,* p.3.

certain negative ones. And like it or not, the responsibility will land back in the lap of medicine and the health-related professions.

To some extent this expansion of medicine into the direct handling of life's problems is self-conscious. I can do little better than cite the 1971 Presidential address of Dr. P. Henderson to the British School Health Service Group.[1] His paper was a clarion call for his fellow school health workers to get involved in the following "health problems":

> Poverty and slum or new slum housing
> Behaviour and emotional difficulties
> Maladjustment
> Juvenile delinquency
> Drug taking
> Suicide
> Children in care
> Venereal diseases
> Teenage illegitimate pregnancies
> Abortion

To these which he singles out for special attention, he adds the more traditional problems of children with visual, hearing, physical handicaps, those with speech and language difficulties, the epileptics, the diabetics, the asthmatics, the dyslexics, the emotionally, the educationally and intellectually retarded. One wonders who or what is left out.

[1] P. Henderson, 'Some Continuing Health Problems of School Children and Young People and Their Implications for a Child and Youth Health Service,' *Public Health London,* Vol. 85, 1971, pp. 58-66.

THE POLITICS OF MEDICALIZATION

All this medicalization has political consequences although we do our best to deny them. There is an ever increasing use of the metaphor, health and illness, as an explanatory variable if not the explanation itself of a host of social problems. A look at the *New York Times* in a recent year yielded medical and psychiatric commentaries on such diverse phenomena as divorces, race riots, black power, juvenile delinquency, racial and religious intermarriage, the users of heroin, LSD and marijuana, college drop-outs, disrespectful children, hippies, civil rights workers, student protesters, anti-war demonstrators, medical critics, non-voters, draft resisters, and female liberationists. I do not wish to argue whether feminists and protesters have clinical maladies. My concern is what happens when a problem and its bearers become tainted with the label "illness". Any emphasis on the latter inevitably locates the source of trouble as well as the place of treatment primarily in individuals and makes the etiology of the trouble asocial and impersonal, like a virulent bacteria or a hormonal imbalance. While this may have a pragmatic basis in the handling of a specific organic ailment when a social problem is located primarily in the individual or his immediate circle, it has the additional function of blinding us to larger and discomfiting truths. As a disease it is by definition not social and at the same time the expected level of intervention is also not social. If it has to be handled anywhere or if anyone is to blame it is individuals—usually the carriers of the problem—and certainly not the rest of us, or society at large. Thus, it is much easier to think of Hitler and the Nazis as a band of sick psychopaths who created World War II and modernized the concept of "genocide" than to question the complicity of 40 million Germans and a world that stood by. So too it is more comforting to speculate on the degree of sickness of Richard Nixon and the misguided neuroticism and paranoia of his cohorts than to ask what kind of social, economic and political system created such people.

Still another appeal of the medical model is its assumed moral neutrality. Herein, however, lies the greatest potentiality for obfuscating moral issues. Illness, in the medical perspective, assumes something painful and undesirable, and thereby something that can and should be eliminated. It is because of the latter element that great caution must be exercised in the equating of social problems or unpleasant social phenomena with illness. For a social illness, like an individual one, is by definition to be eliminated, *regardless* of the wish of the individual.

The word "regardless" is a key element. In the process of labelling a social problem an illness, there is a power imbalance of tremendous import. For illness is only to be diagnosed and treated by certain specified licensed and mandated officials— primarily doctors. In such a situation the potential patient has little right of appeal to the label-diagnosis. In fact when a patient does object to what is being done for him, the social rhetoric once again may obscure the issue, i.e., since he is sick, he does not really know what is good for him, and certainly not whether the behaviour he's engaged in is "worth-while". The treater-diagnosticians, of course, think they *do*, since there is nothing "in it" for them, the experts who made the diagnosis. The very expertise, being socially legitimated, makes this judgement seem morally neutral. It is in such reasoning that there is the greatest deception. Even granting that the illness diagnostician and their tools may be morally neutral, something which I seriously doubt, for society to decide that any particular social problem is relevant to their province is not without moral consequences. This decision is not morally neutral precisely because in establishing its relevance as the key dimension for action, the moral issue is prevented from being squarely faced and occasionally even from being raised. By the very acceptance of a specific behaviour as an illness and the definition of illness as an undesirable state the issue becomes not *whether* to deal with a particular problem but *how* and *when.* Thus, the debate over homosexuality, drugs, abortion, hyperactive children, antisocial behaviour, becomes focussed on the degree of sickness attached to the phenomenon in question (and its carriers) or the extent of *a* "health" risk which *is* involved. And the more principled, more perplexing, or even moral issue of *what* freedom should an individual have over his/her body, or what else, besides the individual, needs treating is shunted aside.

IN CONCLUSION

Basically my contention is that the increasing

use of illness as a lever in the understanding of social problems represents no dramatic shift from a moral view to a neutral one but merely to an alternative strategy. Thus, the shift in the handling of such social problems is primarily in those who will undertake the change (psychiatry and other medical specialities) and where the change will take place (in the individual's psyche and body). The problem being scrutinized and the person being changed is no less immoral for all the medical rhetoric. It or he is still a "problem", though the rhetoric may convince us that he and not the society is responsible, and he not the society should be changed. Even the moral imperatives remain, in the idea that if such a problem-person can be medically-treated-changed, it-he *should* be.

But in addition to the basic depoliticizing effect of the labels "health and illness", there is also an exclusionary one. That the Women's Movement is making its most important inroads in the delivery of medical services is no accident. In a powerful movie called *Taking Our Bodies Back* and an extraordinary book, *Our Bodies, Ourselves*[1] women not only decry what power they have given up but also how biological and supposed health differences have been used to exclude them from many aspects of life. I fear that this phenomenon of "anatomy being destiny" will become even more widespread. Where once one was excluded from jobs because of race, ethnicity, gender, and age, now one will become ineligible for promotion, inappropriate

[1] Boston Women's Health Book Collective, *Our Bodies, Ourselves*, New York: Simon and Schuster, Rev. Ed. 1976.

for work, pushed to early retirement—all on the basis of one's physical status or health. If you do not think ours is already an exclusionary society look at the architectural barriers we have created to exclude full access and participation of our citizens from schools, restaurants, theatres, public buildings, court houses and even private dwellings. Look at the social barriers wherein a youthful and beauty aesthetic makes us repelled by the old or people in any way deformed. Look at the communication barriers that prevent us from talking comfortably with those who are blind and deaf, gazing directly at someone who is facially disfigured, and listening for long to anyone with a speech defect.

The reasons for all this go deep. As long as the deliverers of service are markedly different in gender, economic class, and race from those to whom they offer services, as long as accessibility to medical care is a privilege rather than a right, as long as the highest income groups are health care professionals, as long as the most profit-making enterprises include the pharmaceutical and insurance industries, society is left with the uncomfortable phenomenon of a portion of its population, living, and living well, off the sufferings of others and to some extent even unwittingly having a vested interest in the continuing existence of such problems.

A web of political, economic, and even social psychological forces support this system, and only with awareness can the dismantling begin. It is for all these reasons that I am convinced that the health area is the example *par excellence* of today's identity crisis—what is or will become of the self. It is the battleground not because there are visible threats and oppressors but because they are almost invisible, not because the perspective, tools, and practitioners of medicine and the other helping professions are inherently evil, but because they are not. It is so frightening because there are elements here of the banality of evil so uncomfortably written about by Hannah Arendt.[1] But here the danger is greater for not only is the process masked as a technical, scientific objective one but one done for our own good. In short, the road to a healthist society may well be paved with supposedly good intentions.

[1] Hannah Arendt, *Eichmann in Jerusalem—A Report on the Banality of Evil,* New York, Viking Press, 1963.

JOHN McKNIGHT

Professionalized Service and Disabling Help

The business of modern society is service. Social service in modern society is business.

This fact is reflected in the language employed. Professionals and their managers now speak of educational "products", health "consumers" and a legal "industry". Clients are defined as "markets" and technocrats—an entirely new breed of professionals—are developing methods to "market" services, using business accountancy systems. Computers measure and store psychological "inputs" and family "outputs". There are "units served" and "units of service" and sophisticated economists, statisticians and planners deal with the production and consumption of social services in the same way as the production, consumption and maintenance of physical goods is accounted for. Furthermore, and this is of central importance, every modernized society, whether socialist or capitalist, is marked by the growing percentage of service in its Gross National Product, not only of services such as postal deliveries, catering, car repairs etc, but social services such as marriage guidance, birth control, counselling, education, legal arbitration, care of the young, the adult and the old in all its ramifications, and all that falls under the general heading of social help.

This stage of economic development is distinguished by its unlimited potential since service production has none of the limits imposed by goods production—limits such as natural resources, capital and land. Therefore, the social service business has endless possibilities for expansion as there seems to be no end to the needs for which services can be manufactured.

Modernized nations are therefore best defined as service economies. They are serviced societies and they are peopled with service producers and service consumers—professionals and clients.

The politics of serviced societies are gradually being clarified. Public budgets are becoming strained under the service load. Many national and local governments find themselves involved in the unprecedented politics of deciding between competing services—should we give more to education and less to medicine? Within the service sectors there are equally difficult dilemmas. Should we cut back on tax-paid abortions or should the available money be used for free 'flu vaccine?

These dilemmas are often resolved by the apolitical ideology of service. While old-fashioned politics, rooted in a goods economy, allowed a civic debate as to whether a nation needed more wheat or more steel, more automobiles or more houses, the new service politics is a debate as to whether we should have more doctors or more teachers, more lawyers or more social workers. Politically the question becomes whether we should trade health for learning, or justice for family well-being. These choices create an impossible politics in traditional terms.

While our political traditions make it possible to decide between wheat and steel, it seems politically impossible to decide between health and education because health and education are not alternatives amenable to choices: they are services. Indeed, the allocation of services is so immune to political debate that many governments resolve the dilemma by deciding that we will have less wheat and more education, less steel and more medicine.

This is not to suggest that these choices are correct or incorrect, or even that they define appropriateness. Rather, it is to say that the apolitical nature of service is so pervasive that it is difficult for the public and policy makers to recognize that the creation and allocation of services are the central political issue in many modernized economies.

The political immunity of the services is best understood in terms of the symbolic referent of service.

Services are something one pays for.

The "good" that is paid for is care.

Care is an act that is an expression of love. We say "I care for her more than anyone" or "I am taking care of my mother and father".

Thus, *service* is to *care* which is to *love* and love is the universal, apolitical value.

Symbolically then, the apolitical nature of service depends on its association with the unlimited universality of love. Ask any servicer what is ultimately satisfying about his work and the answer will most commonly be framed in terms of wanting to care for and help people. Press on and the answer is usually that the individual "loves people".

Since love is not a political issue, care is not a policy question and service becomes the one business that is an unlimited, unquestionable and non-political "good".

While this analysis may seem overly symbolic, consider the political use of the language of social service in the United States. When the first major programme to provide governmentally insured medicine was proposed, it was not described as a policy to expand access to and income for the medical system. It was called Medi*care*.

In a recent address the President of the American Federation of Teachers noted that there are thousands of unemployed teachers and a large new supply graduating from teacher training institutions. He dealt with this economic dilemma by noting that large sectors of the society need education—the pre-school, adult and elderly population. In order to meet this "need", he called for a new government programme to guarantee the life-long educational rights of all Americans. He called it Edu*care*.

In the law schools of the United States, law students number forty per cent of all the practising lawyers in the country. A recent study asked the leaders of the American Bar what they thought could be done to ensure that this flood of new lawyers could provide their service and have an adequate income. The most common response was to suggest the need for a publicly supported programme that would guarantee the rights of all people to legal services. The name that was universally applied to such a programme was Judi*care*.

It is clear, therefore, that the word "care" is a potent political symbol. What is not so clear is that its use masks the political interests of servicers. This fact is further obscured by the symbolic link between care and love. The result is that the politico-economic issues of service are hidden behind the mask of love.

Behind that mask is simply the servicer, his systems, techniques and technologies—a business in need of markets, an economy seeking new growth potential, professionals in need of an income.

It is crucial that we understand that this mask of service is *not* a false face. The power of the ideology of service is demonstrated by the fact that most servicers cannot distinguish the mask from their own face. The service ideology is *not* hypocritical because hypocrisy is the false pretence of a desirable goal. The modernized servicer believes in his care and love, perhaps more than even the serviced. The mask is the face. The service ideology is *not* conspiratorial. A conspiracy is a group decision to create an exploitative result. The modernized servicer honestly joins his fellows to create a supposedly beneficial result. The masks are the faces.

In order to distinguish the mask and the face it is necessary to consider another symbol—need.

We say love is a need. Care is a need. Service is a need. Servicers meet needs. People are collections of needs. Society has needs. The economy should be organized to meet needs.

In a modernized society where the major business is service, the political reality is that the central "need" is an adequate income for professional servicers and the economic growth they portend. The masks of love and care obscure this reality so that the public cannot recognize the professionalized interests that manufacture needs in order to rationalize a service economy. Medicare, Educare, Judicare, Socialcare and Psychocare are portrayed as systems to meet need rather than programmes to meet the needs of servicers and the economies they support.

Removing the mask of love shows us the face of servicers who *need* income, and an economic system that *needs* growth. Within this framework, the client is less a person in need than a person who is needed. In business terms, the client is less the consumer than the raw material for the servicing system. In management terms, the client becomes both the output and the input. His essential function is to meet the needs of servicers, the servicing system and the national economy. The central political issue becomes the servicers' capacity to manufacture needs in order to expand the economy of the servicing system.

Within this analytic framework, pejoratives are inappropriate. After all, a serviced society provides an economy, a structure for social organization, and service workers motivated by the ethical values of care and love. If these service system needs are legitimate, clients can be viewed as needed, rather than in need, and we can get on with the business of researching, developing, manufacturing and marketing services without the necessity to project professional need upon citizens. We can deal in political and economic terms with the needs of servicers, freed of the apolitical mask of love.

The problem with this political resolution is political reality. Throughout modernized societies a troublesome question is being raised by the citizenry. In popular terms it is:

Why are we putting so much resource into medicine while our health is not improving?

Why are we putting so much resource into education and our children seem to be learning less?

Why are we putting so much resource into criminal justice systems and society seems less just and less secure?

Why are we putting so much more resource into mental health systems and we seem to have more mental illness?

As if these questions were not troubling enough, a new group of service system critics are asking whether we are putting more resources in and getting out the very opposite of what the system is designed to "produce". In medicine, this question is most clearly defined as iatrogenesis—doctor created disease. The new critics' question is not whether we get less service for more resource. Rather, it is whether we get the reverse of what the service system is supposed to "produce". In the terms of Ivan Illich, the question is whether the systems have become counterproductive. Do we get more sickness from more medicine? Do we get more injustice and crime with more lawyers and police? Do we get more ignorance with more teachers and schools? Do we get more family collapse with more social workers?

This is the question that is most threatening to the previously apolitical service systems because, while services defined as embodiments of care and love are a political platform; while services that are understood as being less effective than they have in the past are a political possibility; while it is even politically feasible to remove the mask of love and recognize services as systems in need of resources in order that economies may grow, it is politically *impossible* to maintain a service economy if the populace perceives that the service system hurts more than it helps—that professional service can become disabling help.

In the last few years, the progressive leaders of the service business have recognized the counter-productive threat. Their response has been to develop new strategies to deal with the counter-productivity of service systems. They have called upon the skills of another profession—the managers. Their assumption is that while professional servicers are unable to control the harm they induce, the managerial profession can become the modern reformer, controlling and directing the systems so that counterproductivity is neutralized, while at the same time protecting the political support for the growth of the service system.

The new service manager, translating his skills from the goods production sector, sees four elements to be manipulated in rationalizing the service system: budgets, personnel, organizational structure and technology. Therefore, the service manager is now busily at work instituting cost control systems, developing personnel training systems, restructuring delivery systems and introducing new technologies.

The most progressive managers have used their advanced marketing skills to develop a fifth manipulation—preparing the client. They recognize that if there is no need for service, it is possible to manufacture a need. If the popular perceptions of need do not fit the service, social service managers have developed techniques that can persuade people to fit the service through advanced marketing systems.

Will these professional management techniques stabilize the service business by eliminating counter-productive effects?

Certainly the capacities of modern management systems are impressive. Aided by the apolitical ideology of the services, one might well prophesy a collaboration between the servicers and their managers to coalesce into an irresistible force that will henceforth direct the economic policies of modernized economies.

An alternative view suggests that there may be a counterbalance—indeed an immovable object—that faces the irresistible force: a new ideology that assigns to the state the coordination of total disservice.

If such an object exists, it is found in the human necessity to act rather than be acted upon; to be citizen rather than client. It is this human imperative that suggest that even the best managed service systems will be unable to overcome popular recognition of the disabling impacts of modernized professional service.

The remainder of this essay attempts to identify the disabling effects of modernized service systems and to suggest the political consequences of the conflict between the irresistible force of client-making and the immovable object of citizen action.

PROFESSIONALIZED ASSUMPTIONS REGARDING NEED

Three disabling effects grow from professional-ized assumptions of need.

First is the translation of a need into a deficiency. A need could be understood as a condition, a want, a right, an obligation of another, an illusion or an unresolvable problem. Professional practice consistently defines a need as an unfortunate absence or emptiness in another.

One is reminded of the child's riddle asking someone to describe a glass that has water in its lower half. Is it half full—or half empty? The basic function of modernized professionalism is to legitimize human beings whose capacity it is to see their neighbour as half empty. Professionalized research increasingly devotes its efforts to extending the upper rim of the glass in order to ensure that it will never be filled—even by the results of "effective service".

In a servicing economy where the majority of the people derive their income from professionalized "helping" and GNP is measured by services rendered, nations need an increased *supply* of personal deficiency. Thus, a society that purports to meet need defined as personal deficiency is more accurately understood as an economy in need of need. The comic distortion could be societies of neighbours whose income depends upon finding the deficiency in each other. The political consequence is neighbours unable to act as communities of competence with the capacity to perceive or act upon solvable problems.

The *second* disabling characteristic of professionalized definitions of need is the professional practice of placing the perceived deficiency *in* the client. While most modernized professionals will agree that individual problems develop in a socio-economic-political context, their common remedial practice isolates the individual from the context. The effect of this individualization leads the professional to distort even his own contextual understanding. Because his remedial tools and techniques are usually limited to individualized interaction, the interpretation of the need necessarily becomes individualized. The tool defines the problem rather than the problem defining the tool.

A recent study of children who became state wards exemplifies the process. The children were legally separated from their families because the parents were judged to be unable to provide adequate care for the children. Therefore, the children were placed in professional service institutions. However, the majority of the professional case records portrayed the children as the problem. Quite correctly, officials who were involved in removing the children from their homes agreed that a common reason for removal was the economic poverty of the family. Obviously, they had no resources to deal with poverty. But there were many resources for professionalized institutional service. The service system met the economic need by institutionalizing an individualized definition of the problem. The negative side effect was that the poverty of the families was intensified by the resources consumed by the "caring" professional services. In counterproductive terms, the servicing system "produced" broken families.

The individualizing, therapeutic definition of need has met a counteracting force in some of the "liberation" movements. The civil rights and women's liberation movements are cases in point. Their essential ideological function is to persuade minorities and women that they are human beings who are neither deficient nor dependent upon systems purporting to meet their "needs" through individualized professional help. Instead, these movements struggle to overcome the individualized deficiency oriented "consciousness" communicated by the professional service ideology by affirming individual competence and collective action.

The *third* disabling effect of professionalized definitions of need results from specialization—the major "product" of advanced systems of technique and technology. We all know that this process creates highly specialized, intricately organized service systems that provide magnificent organizational problems for the new service managers. Vast human and financial resources are now devoted to the rationalization of these systems, providing politically acceptable criteria justifying economic growth through the service sector.

What is less clearly understood is that these systems impose their mirror image on the citizenry. As the systems are a set of managed parts, so the client is necessarily understood and processed as a set of manageable parts, each with its own service mechanic. These complex service systems remind one of those table mats in some restaurants that show a cow divided into parts locating the steak, the roast, the ribs and the tongue.

In like manner, professionalized service definitions increasingly translate need in terms of people in pieces. We need podiatrists for our hooves and Eye, Ear, Nose and Throat men for our snouts. Our psyche, marriage, relationship with our children, in fact our most intimate and personal activities are divided into separate bits and pieces.

Modernized professions also piece us out in time. Service professionals now assure us that we live through a set of needs defined by age. Professionals have "found" seven life crises (formerly known as the seven ages of man) from infancy to death, each requiring its helping professional. Elizabeth Kubler-Ross has advanced the process by giving us five phases of death. Her work ensures a new set of helpers for stage one of dying, stage two of dying, etc. Following these dying therapists will be research professionals attempting to decide why some people skip, say, stage two or three of dying.

While individualizing need may disable by removing people from the social context, the compartmentalization of the person removes even the potential for individual action. People are, instead, a set of pieces in need, both in time and space. Hopefully, the pieces can be put together again to make a human unit of sufficient residual effectiveness to pay for "its" servicing.

To sum up, professionalized services define need as a deficiency and at the same time individualize and compartmentalize the deficient components. The service systems communicate three propositions to the client:

> You are deficient
>
> You are the problem
>
> You have a collection of problems

In terms of the interest of service systems and their *needs,* the propositions become:

> We *need* deficiency
>
> The economic unit we *need* is individuals
>
> The productive economic unit we *need* is an individual with multiple deficiencies

THE PROFESSIONALIZED ASSUMPTIONS REGARDING THE REMEDY OF NEED

These professionalized definitions of need produce a logical and necessary set of remedial assumptions, each with its own intrinsically disabling effects.

The *first* of these assumptions is the mirror image of the individualized definition of need. As *you* are the problem, the assumption is that *I,* the professionalized servicer, *am the answer. You* are not the answer. *Your peers* are not the answer. *The political, social and economic environment* is not the answer. Nor is it possible that there is no answer. I, the professional, am the answer. The central assumption is that service is a unilateral process. I, the professional, produce. You the client, consume.

There are, of course, an impressive set of professionalized coping mechanisms that have been developed by sensitive servicers to deny the unilateral nature of professionalized service. They are described as group-orientated services, peer-orientated services, client-orientated services, and community-orientated services. Each of these rhetorical devices is a symbolic attempt to deal with the anxieties of servicers who *need* to deny the unilateral nature of their relationships.

While it is clear that many humanistic professionals seek a democratic definition for their role, it is difficult to perceive the bilateral component beyond the clients' payment, whether out of pocket or through taxation. Indeed, a basic definition of "unprofessional conduct" is "becoming involved with the client". To be professional is to distance—to ensure that the relationship is defined in terms that allow the client to understand who is *really* being serviced.

In spite of the democratic pretence, the disabling function of unilateral professional help is the hidden assumption that "You will be better because I, the professional, know better".

The political implications of this assumption are central to anti-democratic systems. Indeed, it is possible that societies, dependent on economies of unilateral professional servicing, are systematically preparing their people for anti-democratic leaders who can capitalize upon the dependencies created by expert, professionalized helpers, who teach people that "they will be better because we, the professional helpers, know better".

A *second* disabling characteristic of professionalized remedial assumptions is the necessity for the remedy to define the need. As professionalized service systems create more elegant techniques and magnificent tools, they create an imperative demanding their use.

The problem with these beautiful, shiny, complex, professional tools and techniques is that their "benefits" are not easily comprehended by the public. Therefore, we see the professions developing internal logics and public marketing systems that assure use of the tools and techniques by assuming that the client doesn't understand what he needs. Therefore, if the client is to have the benefit of the professional remedy, he must also understand that the professional not only knows what he needs but also knows how the need is to be met.

Thus the complex professional remedial tools have come to justify the professional power to define the need—to decide not only the appropriate remedy but the definition of the problem itself. Increasingly, professions assume that in order to deal with deficiency, they must have the prerogative to decide what is deficient.

There is no greater power than the right to define the question. From that right flows a set of necessary answers. If the servicer can effectively assert the right to define the appropriate question, he has the power to determine the need of his neighbour rather than meeting his neighbour's need.

While this power allows the professional to use his shiny new remedy, it also defines citizens as people who can't understand whether they have a problem—much less what should be done about it.

Modernized societies are now replete with need-defining research. Professionals have recently "discovered" tool-using needs called child abuse, learning disabilities and, "removal trauma" (the need for therapy for children who are traumatized because they are removed from their alledgedly traumatic families). Brigitte Berger suggests, in a recent article, that baldness will soon be defined as a disease because underemployed dermatologists will decree it to be one. The final institutionalization of the process is a new programme developed by a famous clinic in the United States: the programme provides a costly opportunity for people who don't feel anything is wrong to find out what problems they have that meet the needs of new tools.

When the capacity to define the problem becomes a professional prerogative, citizens no longer exist. The prerogative removes the citizen as problem-definer, much less problem-solver. It translates political functions into technical and technological problems.

Once the service professional can define remedy and need, a *third* disabling remedial practice develops. It is the coding of the problem and the solution into languages that are incomprehensible to citizens.

While it is clearly disabling to be told you can't decide whether you have a problem and how it can be dealt with, the professional imperative compounds the dilemma by demonstrating that you couldn't understand the problem or the solution anyway. The language of modernized professional services mystifies both problem and solution so that citizen evaluation becomes impossible. The only people "competent" to decide whether the servicing process has any merit are professional peers, each affirming the basic assumptions of the other.

While there are fascinating inter-jurisdictional disputes among servicing peers, these conflicts rarely break the rule that it is only the professional who understands the problem and the solution. The internal conflicts are power struggles over which professionals shall be dominant. A professional who breaks the rule of professional dominance will be stigmatized by all the disputants and loses his place on the rungs of the ladder to success. The politics of modernized professional power is bounded by peer review. Modern heretics are those professional practitioners who support citizen competence and convert their profession into an understandable trade under the comprehensible command of citizens.

The critical disabling effect of professional coding is its impact upon citizen capacities to deal with cause and effect. If I cannot understand the question or the answer—the need or the remedy—I exist at the sufference of expert systems. My world is not a place where I do or act with others. Rather, it is a mysterious place, a strange land beyond my comprehension or control. It is understood only by professionals who know *how* it works, *what* I need and *how* my need is met. I am the object rather than the actor. My very being is as client rather than citizen. My life and our society are technical problems rather than political systems.

As the service professions gain the power to unilaterally define remedy, need, and code the service process, a *fourth* disabling characteristic develops. It is the capacity of servicers to define the output of their service in accordance with their own satisfaction with the result. This fourth capacity develops in a service profession just as the citizen is totally and definitely transmogrified into a *critical* addict.

Increasingly, professionals are claiming the power to decide whether their "help" is effective. The important, valued and evaluated outcome of service is the professional's assessment of his own efficacy. The client is viewed as a deficient person, unable to know whether he has been helped.

This developing professional premise is contested by the consumer movement. The movement is a valiant last stand of those disabled citizens who lay final claim to the right to evaluate the effects or "outputs" of professionalized service.

The basic assumption of the movement is that citizens are enabled because they have become powerful consumers. In this assumption the movement is a handmaiden of the serviced society. It implicitly accepts the service ideology. Citizens *are* as they consume. Citizen welfare is defined by equitable, efficacious consumption. The service system is a given good. The citizen role is in evaluating the output. While citizens may not understand the service system, the consumer movement assumes they do know whether the system's output helps or hurts.

Professionally managed service systems are now dealing with this remnant citizen role as consumer. The result has been an increasing professional focus on manipulating consumer perceptions of outcomes. Thomas Dewar, in a paper titled *The Professionalization of the Client,* describes how the service systems are training citizens to understand that their satisfaction is derived from being effective clients rather than people whose problems are solved.

The paradigm of this process is the school. Unlike most servicing systems, the school is transparent in its institutional definition of the client's role. The school client is evaluated in terms of his ability to satisfy the teacher. The explicit outcome of the system is professional approval of behaviour and performance.

The professional imperative is now universalizing the ideology of the school, communicating the value of effective clienthood. Negating even the client "output" evaluation, modernized professional services increasingly communicate the value of being an effective client as the proof of the system's efficacy.

Once effective "clienthood" becomes a central

value in society, the consumer movement as we know it now· will be stifled and will wither away.

The service ideology will be consummated when citizens believe that they cannot know whether they have a need, cannot know what the remedy is, cannot understand the process that purports to meet the need or remedy and cannot even know whether the need is met unless professionals express satisfaction. The ultimate sign of a serviced society is a professional saying, "I'm so pleased by what you've done". The demise of citizenship is to respond, "Thank you".

We will have reached the apogee of the modernized service society when the professionals can say to the citizen:

>We are the solution to your problem.
>
>We know what problem you have.
>
>You can't understand the problem or the solution.
>
>Only we can decide whether the solution has dealt with your problem.

Inverted, in terms of the needs of professionalized service systems, these propositions become:

>We *need* to solve your problems.
>
>We *need* to tell you what they are.
>
>We *need* to deal with them in our terms.
>
>We *need* to have you respect our satisfaction with our own work.

The most important research issues in modernized societies involve an understanding of the *needs* of servicers and the mechanics of their systems. These systems are obviously important. They provide incomes for a majority of the people. They support national economies. It is, of course, no secret that they are consistently failing to meet their own goals in spite of magnanimous applications of money and personnel. It is becoming more and more evident that rather than *producing* "services" they are creating sensitive but frustrated professionals, unable to understand why their love, care and service does not re-form society, much less help individuals to function.

We should, therefore, reorient our research efforts toward the needs of servicers. After all, they are a growing majority of people employed in modernized societies and they are an increasingly sad, alienated class of people in *need* of support, respect, care and love. Modernized societies *need* to determine how we can help these professionalized servicers while limiting their power to disable the capacities of citizens to perceive and deal with issues in political terms.

And if we cannot do that we should at least understand the political impact of the disabling nature of professionalized definitions of need and remedy.

Professionalized services .communicate a world view that defines our lives and our societies as a series of technical problems. This technical definition is masked by symbols of care and love that obscure the economic interests of the servicers and the disabling characteristics of their practices.

The sum of these disabling characteristics is an ideology that converts citizens to clients, communities to deficient individuals and politics to a self-serving debate by professionals over which service system should have a larger share of the Gross National Product.

The foregoing analysis is *not* an argument for the reform of professionalized service in order to remove the disabling effects. Rather, the analysis suggests that the disabling effects are intrinsic to modernized professionalized service. Whatever benefits they might provide can only be assessed after we recognize them as essentially self-interested systems with inherently disabling effects. Within this framework, the political definition of a citizen can be restored. The inherently disabling effects of professionalized services can be assessed and balanced against their possible benefits. Policies can be developed that select those service benefits that overbalance the intrinsically disabling effects.

In the meantime, the politics of modernized societies will be the conflict between the irresistible resistance of the service business and the immovable object created by citizens who have experienced the disabling help of privileged professional servicers who wear the mask of love.

JONATHAN CAPLAN

Lawyers and Litigants:
A Cult Reviewed

The easiest way to create a monopoly is to invent
a language and procedure which will be unintelli-
gible to the layman. This illusion of complexity—
whose grand finale, like a rabbit out of a hat, is the
divination of simplicity—has, in the past, been the
art of countless quacks. In many ways, it is also
the art of the ancient and noble profession of the
law.

The extent of the monopoly is awe-inspiring. We
have handed over to a professional corps more
power than we would give to any elected executive.
We have done it unquestioningly and largely

unknowingly and even now call for no supervision or checks and balances in return. It is a monopoly which touches our daily lives at every point imaginable: it fashions our education, our relationships and even our morals. This transference of power to the lawyers has slipped through smoothly because of our respect for the law.

Though positivist and man-made, the law—in the words of Thurman Arnold—is 'a great reservoir of emotionally important social symbols'. The law is the leveller in our society: before it, all are equal and all may go in search of justice. Its regulation of human behaviour—enforced by sanction—is our only barrier between ordered civilization and anarchy.

This respect for the law inevitably invests those engaged in its practice with a certain amount of power. The administration of human affairs, even the most routine, is now in the firm grip of lawyers. It is traditional to celebrate almost every milestone in one's life—such as buying a house, getting a divorce, making a will—by a visit to a lawyer, as if we have been schooled to seek double consecration by Church and advocate. It is the idea in practice that lawyers are indispensable if things are not to go wrong.

Until very recently, the assumption that law was necessary led uncritically to the assumption that lawyers too were necessary. State legal aid and the mushrooming of local law firms and advice centres permitted classless indulgence in recourse to the lawyer. Legal assistance was held to be as important as hospital assistance and the professional determination of one's rights as paramount as any medical check-up.

Legal assistance became an obsession and the obsession became a superstition. "Unless a lawyer does my conveyancing, my house will turn out not to belong to me: unless a lawyer writes a letter on my behalf, I will not get any money". But quickly the superstition became a profitable monopoly that was reinforced by the state and citizen's advice bureaux and, in most jurisdictions, the monopoly has passed unquestioned. In England, for example, the Solicitors Act 1957 actually wards off legally unqualified competitors—in the fields of conveyancing and wills by the threat of criminal prosecution.

Moreover, the role of the lawyer is ever encroaching into new spheres. As one of the service professions, it is remarkable that lawyers have escaped scrutiny for so long. The moves towards do-it-yourself law and commissions of inquiry into lawyers' services are relatively new. Even then, however, they do not really begin to expose the roots of the profession's influence.

AN UNRESTRICTED ROLE

The most common attack levelled against the lawyers is Marxist in origin. It is the control of property, the argument goes, that leads to the control of resources and of human beings, and by such devices as their concept of property, the right of ownership, and the doctrine of possession, lawyers rigorously preserve the status quo and act as a powerful force against social change.

Political criticisms certainly can be made of lawyers but this one is unfair because it mistakes the role of the lawyer which, whatever it may be, cannot be said to be legislative in character. It is for the legislature in democratic assembly to effect social change, not the lawyer by personal whim.

This Marxist error underlines the problem. There has been a complete lack of any attempt to define the lawyer's role and the failure to attempt such inquiry or definition has meant that lawyers have been free to range unchecked into ever wider spheres and fields of activity. As soon as a new field of human endeavour or interest is established as a commercial proposition, the lawyers move in to secure their role and profess their expertise. More recently this has happened with industrial relations (which is utterly unsuited to the legal process) and sexual equality.

The highpoint of the lawyer's claim to supervise human affairs is well put in the following assertion made by Lord Macmillan in his book "The Ethics of Advocacy":

> 'The existence of a class of trained advocates possessing knowledge in the law, skill in the orderly presentation of facts, cogency in legal argument and fairness and moderation in controversy is indispensable'.

In the daily promotion of consumer products and commercial services, we are used to hardsell advertising and we even rely on it to narrow an otherwise limitless field of choice. Perhaps this is a part of the reason why, when we encounter such statements in different contexts—here in the service profession of the law, we more readily accept them. We are told lawyers are indispensable and, since we have no clear idea of what lawyers do, we accept it.

The great difference, however, between a lawyer

and a tin of peas is that we do not always know when and whether we need one, nor, since a lawyer's performance is largely ritualistic expertise, is consumer criticism normally possible; even if it is, we cannot appeal to an independent supervising agency but only to a professional governing body. The legal profession, therefore, has none of the checks by which we measure other consumer services. If need and performance cannot be assessed, and if service hire is virtually required by the system, the monopoly is both furthered and entrenched.

COUNTERFEIT HIRE

Do we need a lawyer? In any system of criminal justice the answer is unqualifiably that we do. But in relation to every other issue—that is to say, every non-criminal matter—the role of the lawyer should be open to question. Of course, there are many situations in which we require legal advice but in a host of others lawyers are indiscriminately hired on the grounds of need when the need is, in reality, not a need at all and either a subterfuge for some other motive or a surrender to the consequences of not having a lawyer.

The second half of the twentieth century is the age when experts were revered and when expert advice became an expensive commodity. For the professions this was a Klondike since all professional advice passes as expert. But legal advice is not invariably expert. 'A good deal of the lawyer's competence', said Dietrich Rueschmeyer, 'is connected with his legal knowledge only indirectly or not at 'all' ("Doctors and Lawyers: a comment on the theory of the professions." Canadian Review of Sociology and Anthropology 1964, pp 17-30).

To "seek legal advice" may, therefore, cover a multitude of situations none of which necessarily arise from the need to consult a lawyer at all. Frequently legal advice is simply common sense or experience of the kind of which most rational people are capable, yet we choose to pay lawyers for the reassurance of involving some intelligent third party in our personal affairs. In such a way, we consult lawyers as a lovesick teenager would consult an agony columnist. To gain an ally at a time of doubt or distress. To have an audience with someone who is dispassionate. It might just as well be an unqualified neighbour or someone from a completely different discipline such as a social worker or psychiatrist. But it is traditionally the lawyer because the whole process of consultation has been made respectable and is euphemistically called "seeking legal advice". Society does not attach any hang-up to visiting a lawyers' office.

A combination of supernatural belief and carefully induced prudence accounts for another large slice of lawyers' business. Lawyers heal situations, ward off trouble, and make problems disappear. This reposition of faith has all the symptoms of a cult which has so permeated the consciousness of society that it has lost its fringe quality. The chief sponsors of the "pygmalion" process have been the legislative assemblies and the courts who have encouraged the use of lawyers in a number of ways which are discussed later. It is a cult founded from the popular viewpoint on the fear of the consequences of not having a lawyer, and from the official viewpoint on the paternalistic belief that people ought to be assisted. As a general proposition—with the exception of criminal issues—this is misguided and wasteful.

In the majority of legal consultations, all that a lawyer does is to elicit the facts and then to re-state the client's position in terms of legal rights and duties so as to highlight the strengths and weaknesses of the case. Like a soothsayer of the law, a lawyer predicts a court's reaction to a given situation. His experience and judgement may often be invaluable, but much more often this mere stating of the odds is unnecessary and people could help themselves equally well if only they were educated and encouraged to do so.

The truth is that, nine times out of ten, cases are decided not on a point of law but solely on their facts and the merits. Judges rationalize their con-clusion of what is just in the circumstances from the evidence before them: they do not deduce it from rules and legal precedent. Judicial reasons, as Professor Wisdom has said, 'are like the legs of a chair, not the links in a chain'. They support but hardly ever dictate* what it is wanted to say. The law in practice is not so formalistic that it places the judiciary in straitjackets: the process of judicial decision is controlled discretion. In virtually every contested case that comes before a court some kind of value judgement is made in the process of deciding it—even if it is only in the way that the judge frames the issues of fact for decision. 'Values', said Mr. Justice Holmes in the United States Supreme Court, 'are the inarticulate major premise of judicial reasoning.'

The point is that it is almost always the facts and the merits that will decide. The late Lord Reid, a distinguished member of the appellate committee in the House of Lords, used to advise extra-judicially not to waste time arguing law but to establish a case on its merits as quickly as possible. It is precisely the facts and the merits which are best known to the litigant himself, and a large part of the cost of all legal consultancy is accounted for by the time it takes simply to explain them to a lawyer so that he can repeat them at a later stage. Yet facts can, in the course of such re-telling, lose their force or cogency and litigants in many cases might do better in presenting their cause themselves and in establishing the merits. Clearly if there was a move towards a more informal committee-like court structure, litigants would have the option to do so.

THE CONSEQUENCES OF NOT HAVING A LAWYER.

There are very few vexatious litigants. Most people come into contact with the legal process only once if at all in their lifetime, usually either in the wake of some personal crisis or as a result of a heated dispute in the course of their business. In such circumstances, most potential litigants are acutely vulnerable. They go to law only to win and not to criticize the legal establishment. They, therefore, play the system uncritically.

It is a popular belief that you will not be able to do justice to your own case unless a lawyer represents you. It is the medieval tradition that justice is only achieved through a battle of retained champions. Without a lawyer, you deem yourself—and, above all, are deemed by others—to have no ammunition and no real status as a complainant. Against elusive business customers or an impossible neighbour, a lawyer offers himself as a legalized strongman: like protection rackets, the bigger the firm the more seriously you are taken.

Legal systems give no confidence to litigants to go it alone. They call for dependence on lawyers. The complexity of pre-trial procedure, the ritualized style of pleadings, the public arena of the court—all contribute to make the pursuit of even the most simple claim a professional venture. We are not educated to cope: school syllabuses contain nothing which gives even a hint about what to do or expect. Left alone, people are unsure of their rights and even more unsure of how to press for them.

Most legal systems are not geared to cope with litigants in person who are usually categorized as eccentrics who selfishly bring delay and chaos to an otherwise smooth administration of justice. Lawyers representing the other side will generally not communicate as easily or as frankly with a litigant in person as they would with another lawyer: judges also communicate less effectively with litigants in person perhaps because they feel a duty to be more cautious and feel that they are too personally involved to be capable of objective dialogue. There is a grave risk, therefore, that a litigant representing himself will not be able to get into the best position for negotiation before trial or to manoeuvre to his best advantage at trial. In this curious way, it may

101

be that our legal systems have made representation the prerequisite to complete justice.

RE-INFORCING THE CULT

Our reliance on, and indiscriminate hire of, lawyers is induced in several ways.

Firstly, as Lord Devlin has pointed out, instead of creating a "self service cafeteria", it has been the mistake of every legal system to insist upon "waiter service". A country's legal system is its showpiece, its reference in international credibility. But the expense is crippling and the merits of such a service to the paying client and the taxpayer are open to serious question. It is a monopoly that we ought not to be sure we even require. The great risk of unnecessary consultation is that it frequently leads to unnecessary litigation.

Secondly, the complexity of the provisions that are weekly being legislated to regulate our commercial and even social relationships, not to mention environmental obligations, is such that our law is rapidly resembling some enigmatic code. Much of the drafting of present-day legislation is couched is such obscurity that it requires professional code-breakers and probably goes through on the premise that they will be consulted as a matter of course. Dependence is powerful fuel to any cult; in relation to the legal profession, it is founded on the propogation of the idea—promoted by our legislative assemblies—that laymen can only view the law through a glass darkly. Professionals must interpret and apply it.

Thirdly, the universal insistence that, since the law requires respect, the determination of legal issues should be fought out in a ritualistic and formalized atmosphere. Courts are arenas run on ceremony and form rather than committee-rooms practising a reassuring but firm informality. It is as if justice and respect for the law demands such ritual, but the trappings serve only to invest the legal process with all the mystique of a religion instead of presenting it simply as a code which we apply to regulate social and commercial behaviour and to resolve conflict.

Fourthly, there is a total failure to provide facilities for litigants in person. Although everyone is presumed to know the law, they are not educated or encouraged to understand it or to apply it. It is the lawyers who solve our problems and who, like the high priesthood, alone are familiar with the workings of the legal machine.

Finally, having brought about the various factors inducing dependence, the monopoly is made complete by the comparatively recent introduction of state legal aid. Consultation is easier, indiscriminate hire more probable, the cult re-inforced.

An important part of the cult is relegating the role of the litigant. Litigants are usually only tolerated, and their role confined to that of bystanders and witnesses. It is as if the legal process is some vast and creaking machine which, once set in motion, cannot be approached or operated except by those who have been initiated in its workings.

Most litigants are required to surrender complete control of their case to the lawyers on the ground that they do not know what is best for them, and meekly accept relegation to the position of observer in a drama which could radically alter their lives. Although lawyers claim to act only on instructions, that is only the literal truth and not the reality.

Law is a service profession: in England, a service tax is levied on lawyers' services. Like a client in any other situation, litigants ought, therefore—at the very least—to have consumer rights. They should be able to shop around, know the kind of service they ought to be getting, and be able both to question and measure it according to accepted standards. Yet the induced dependence on lawyers is so great, that they commonly abdicate not only consumer rights but even residual supervision.

THE JUDICIAL CONSEQUENCE

With the exception of armed conflict, virtually every manner of crisis in our society is fought out in the courts. Political confrontations and moral debates are settled finally by the legal profession once most of the headline heat has cooled. The Chicago Seven, the Angry Brigade, Baader-Meinhof, Brown -v- the Board of Education, the English prosecution of the Schoolkids' Oz, the American trial of Ralph Ginzburg—the constitutional and criminal cases are replete with examples. The very pulse of our society, of its direction and its out-bursts, falls to be examined by the legal process. Every surge forward is either checked or en-couraged.

It is this ability to examine which produces the

most penetrating consequence of the lawyer's monopoly. It is the judicial consequence. The fact that lawyers are the sole candidates eligible for the judiciary. The members of this small élite do not merely condemn and sentence, but, by a fine continuous thread of judgements, actually fashion our social standards and set the bounds of our public morality. The judge is—to use a phrase coined by Lord Mansfield in the eighteenth century and cited with approval by the appellate committee of the House of Lords as recently as 1961—the "custos morum" of the people.

But his power goes even further. In most jurisdictions, the judiciary will pronounce on the very legality of the acts of the democratically elected executive to the point of striking down a statute. It is the judiciary who interpret constitutions, claim the power to review the policies of administrations, and even declare or deny the legality of governments to govern.

The scope of their power and its implications is only fully appreciated when it is realized that they pass into power—by mere appointment—unquestioned and usually unknown. What other career would we tolerate whose promotion prospects carried such omnipotence without, at the very least, insisting upon the closest public scrutiny? Who are these men and what are their qualifications? Do they have prejudices, and, if so, are they coincident with our interests?

The identity of the judiciary and its politics is important because it is the judiciary's sense of *Zeitgeist* which runs through judicial precedent and which, together with legislation, provides the blueprint for our social development. It is the judiciary's sense of fairness and propriety which sets our standards and those of public administration.

The judicial consequence implies judicial discretion. Benjamin Cardozo, an Associate Justice of the United States Supreme Court in the thirties, put it vividly:

'We do not pick our rules of law full blossomed from the trees. Every judge consulting his experience must be conscious of times when a free exercise of will, directed of set purpose to the furtherance of the common good, determined the form and tendency of a rule which at that moment took its origin in one creative act') *(The Nature of the Judicial Process* pp 103-4: Yale University Press).

A little earlier, on December 8th 1908 to be exact, President Roosevelt had stated it more bluntly in his message to Congress:

'The chief lawmakers in our country may be, and often are, the judges, because they are the final seat of authority. Every time they interpret contract, property, vested rights, due process of law, liberty, they necessarily enact into law parts of a system of social philosophy; and as such interpretation is fundamental, they give direction to all lawmaking. The decisions of the courts on economic and social questions depend upon their economic and social philosophy; and for the peaceful progress of our people during the twentieth century, we shall owe most to those judges who hold to a twentieth century economic and social philosophy and not to a long outgrown philosophy which was itself the product of primitive economic conditions' (43 Congressional Record: Part 1 page 21).

In 1908, such jurisprudence attracted outraged criticism. Many people then and now perhaps do not care to contemplate the judicial consequence and the fact that we repose such total trust and power in a group of men who have simply reached the pinnacle of their profession. They prefer to think of justice as being a set of rules which is objectively applied. Yet once it is appreciated that this is not so, it becomes clear that the service profession of the law is, in every sense, the spawning ground of hidden government.

REVIEWING THE PURSUIT OF JUSTICE

Any advanced legal system ought to be quite clear about the role of the lawyer within it. When the trend is towards increasing independence from manpower, it ought to be questioned why our dependence on the professions, particularly the legal profession, remains unrelieved.

Justice is a demanding ideal and the concept of "computer justice" is generally condemned as abhorrent. Each case carries its own variables and only careful evaluation can strike a proper balance. Any attempt, therefore, at a critical review of the pursuit of justice and how it is best obtained inevitably stirs up deep sensitivities.

The prerequisite to such review ought to be an examination of the laywer's role. Limits to the role should be roughly drawn so that exceeding them is recognized as trespass and not the province of the lawyer. Counterfeit hire should be shown to be counterfeit and there should be massive re-education about the use of lawyers. It is largely a question of slaying myths and allaying fears.

Removing dependence on professionals requires encouragement to help oneself. In the field of law, such encouragement can only be provided by adapting the legal system which, at virtually every stage, currently re-inforces the cult of dependence. Perhaps the starting point would be to strip the law of its majestic image and to dispense so far as possible with the full panoply of legal proceedings. Solutions to human affairs ought to be worked out in a human atmosphere and not an orators' arena baited with procedural traps. The drift towards complexity by our legislative assemblies should also be checked: there is no merit in obscurity or in over-legislating, and the more complex and obscure we make our legal systems, the more firmly entrenched are those professionals who alone claim to understand it. Our dependence on them becomes as hooked as any addict's, and the cost to the State of subsidizing such dependence will soon be crippling if we allow it to continue uncritically. That is, of course, not to say that those who genuinely require assistance should be deprived of it.

There should be a move towards boardroom justice—a justice which is committee-like and which operates informally. Litigants in person should be encouraged and received tolerantly. Legal rights and how to assess them should be taught—at least in outline—in our schools so that initiation no longer comes solely through experience. Compendiums for easy reference on various branches of the law should be compiled and kept up to date with the use of supplements: a library service of those compendiums should be available at every court. Litigants could then generally present their own cases concentrating on the facts and the merits, and leaving, if necessary, any points of law to be spotted and decided by the tribunal. If they felt aggrieved and chose to appeal, then they should at that stage seek legal advice, but the idea that it is invariably necessary to consult a lawyer—and to have him as a representative at any consequent proceedings—ought to be dispelled. In a boardroom system, the consequences of not having a lawyer ought not to result in unfairness or prejudice. Depending on the category of case, it could be an accepted norm.

Our reliance, however, on the quality and impartiality of the "chairmen" or judiciary—whose task it would be to staff such a system—would be greatly increased. There is no desirable way of checking the judicial consequence except to devise a satisfactory method of close public review before judicial appointment and to encourage the use of experts from other fields to sit with a judge as lay advisers: the legislature should also be vigilant and prepared to correct unacceptable judicial precedent by legislation.

To a very large extent, it is, and must be, a matter of trust. But that trust will run much deeper if we are not subject to a legal profession on terms which we do not fully appreciate and which are not really in the public interest.

HARLEY SHAIKEN

Craftsman into Baby Sitter

Some of my most vivid memories of growing up
in Detroit in the early 1950's are waking up at five
in the morning to see my grandfather off to his
job at the mammoth Ford Rouge plant. In case we
forgot the purpose of those ten or eleven tiring
hours my grandfather was away from home, Vice
President Nixon and other luminaries would appear
on TV to remind us that we Americans have the
highest standard of living in the world. In fact, we
were assured that hard work could raise this standard
yet higher by providing us with even more "needed
goods".

111

What TV was not telling us is that after a certain point higher consumption could mean a *lower* quality of life: more automobiles to carry workers farther and farther to meaningless jobs; TV to reproduce a wasteland in colour rather than in black and white, suburban homes to provide an escape from congested cities on even more congested freeways. In the process we lost the ability to walk, communicate with each other, and to live in a community instead of a subdivision.

In short, human activities have become fragmented, unrelated to one another and, most importantly, disjoined from living itself—they have become commodities. No one in industrial society suffers more from this fragmentation than industrial workers. We pay a double price: we sacrifice our lives on the job to obtain demeaned leisure.

I will examine the degradation of work and the way this degrades life by looking at industrial work at its best: skilled work and the more sophisticated attempts to enrich production work. By viewing work at its best, we can most clearly see how capitalism moulds the work process and defines the worker's role in it. The very meaning of work changes from an activity or achievement into a wage relation whose purpose is the maximum extraction of profit. Capitalism, however, is not alone in subordinating human needs to production—it is a common feature of all industrial societies, whatever their ideological creeds.

In looking at industrial work at its best, we see a seemingly contradictory process taking place: skilled work is fragmented and degraded while production work is "widened" and "enriched".

In reality, both processes attempt to control and integrate workers more effectively into a social relation which dominates them. Both processes are a response to the spirit of independence and actual rebelliousness of workers who haven't forgotten that they are human. The purpose of work remains the production of commodities rather than the creation of use value for the workers and society.

The degradation of work is rooted in industrial society itself. In order to make work a creative and meaningful part of life it is necessary to create a society in which people control the productive process democratically by deciding what, how, when and for what purpose production takes place. This presupposes developing a production process that, in fact, *can* be controlled.

Skilled work gives us some unusual insights into how the worker becomes limited and dominated by the work process. There are certainly other aspects of work that present a glaring condemnation of the way this system organizes work: we could speak about coal miners suffering from black lung, or chemical workers becoming paralyzed from nerve damage as a result of handling chemicals, or the boredom of the assembly line. When we talk about the crushing monotony of the assembly line, however, it is the assembly line that appears as the culprit; but when we talk about skilled work it is not the nature of the craft, but the social relation of the worker to management that is under discussion. The full expression of the worker's skill conflicts directly with the needs of management.

Skilled work can be satisfying because it is varied, challenging and creative. It begins far beyond where most job enrichment programmes for unskilled work leave off. Let's take my trade, machining, as an example. You learn certain basic types of operations, each simple and relatively easy to learn, and you combine them with an indefinable ingredient, your own skill, to create what is often a tribute to your vision and experience. Being a skilled machinist eliminates the division between manual and mental labour. One of the real satisfactions of skilled work is that, like an artist, your hands produce what your mind conceives. Today more and more of the work process is being organized to limit your vision to the narrowest possible execution of someone else's plans. If Michelangelo, for example, had to paint in this way, he would have painted the Sistine Chapel by numbers, filling in the colours of someone's neatly laid-out design, or perhaps it would have been more efficient to have Michelangelo do all the blues, and have co-workers apply the other colours.

I've seen first hand how arbitrary the fragmentation of skilled work is by working in a small innovative shop in research and development where a good machinist often does the work of an engineer and an engineer experiments as a machinist. After all, the great pioneers of the industrial revolution came out of the metal working trades rather than the universities. People like Maudslay, or Whitworth or Stephenson or even James Watt came out of the crafts rather than the colleges.

When skilled work is challenging and creative in this way it relies heavily on the judgement and competence of the individual craftsman. To the extent that his skill gives him pride, it also provides a certain level of independence. However, it is precisely this independence that industry seeks to subvert; how can you control labour costs and maximize profits when an important segment of the work force has a high degree of independence? In order to limit this independence, managements have taken a number of important steps, usually in the socially neutral name of "efficiency", that have degraded skilled work. First, planning and engineering are separated from the actual machine work itself. The strict division of the work process into machinists, technicians, and engineers is a social imperative to centralize control rather than a technical necessity. Final control doesn't reside with the engineer, it remains with the manager, whose role is that of a glorified pimp who is anxious to manage the services of the engineer as call girl and the machinist as street walker. Frederick W. Taylor, the father of scientific management, candidly described the reality of industry today when he strongly urged that 'all possible brain work should be removed from the shop and centered in the planning or laying-out department . . .' The word manage, itself, came into English from the Italian word "maneggiare" which meant "to handle and train horses".

Furthermore, since there is still an important degree of autonomy left in deciding how to carry out management's instructions, the machining trade is often broken down into its most basic elements: the lathe, the mill, the grinder, etc. The "all-round" machinist whose job it was to translate a conception into a finished product becomes the operator of a single machine. Here we cease talking about people, or even workers—instead we need "hands". Companies advertise for a "lathe hand" or a "mill hand" because that is exactly what they need—a pair of hands to operate a machine. Since the rest of the worker comes along with the hands, the whole package is tolerated, but it is the hands that are essential.

Finally, new processes such as numerical control or computer control, in which a pre-programmed tape or computer programme determine exactly what the machine will do, put whatever discretionary powers that remained with the worker in the hands of the manager. The skilled worker is demoted from a cog in the production process into a baby sitter for a machine. Like any baby sitter, the machinist is allowed to feed his subject, watch it, and clean up after it.

Iron Age, an important management weekly in the metal working field, described the full significance of the machinist as baby sitter:

> 'Numerical control is more than a means of controlling a machine. It is a system, a method of manufacturing. It embodies much of what the father of scientific management, Frederick Winslow Taylor, sought back in 1880 when he began his investigations into the art of cutting metal.
>
> "Our original objective," Mr. Taylor wrote, "was that of taking the control of the machine shop out of the hands of the many workmen, and placing it completely in the hands of management, thus superseding rule-of-thumb by scientific control." '

The effect of this degradation of skilled workers

was brought home to me by a friend in Detroit when he said: 'Do you know what they are doing to the trade? Why, they're trying to make it nothing but a job!' When a skilled worker today is asked what he does, he may say 'I work for General Motors' rather than 'I am a machinist'. This is because he feels his primary relation on the job is to the corporation rather than to his craft.

As a society we are left with the enormous contradiction between the unique and varied intelligence that constitutes a person and the "hand" that industry wants to carry out its work. A machinist might require constant supervision by management to produce the bare minimum during his shift at work, giving the impression that even stricter supervision would be necessary for more production. Yet the same worker goes home and works until two o'clock in the morning in his garage making parts for his motorcycle at a rate of speed that would displace half of the machinists at work (were it applied), and with a quality that would virtually eliminate the need for an inspection division.

In this example, the type of work being done is the same, but the *relation* is different. In the factory, the worker executes a plan he had no role in formulating, often as part of a work process that does its best to relate to him as a mere pair of hands, for a product he has little or no relation to, and for which he sees only an indirect benefit for himself. The frustration of not being able to apply his skills on the job is often the motivation for doing it at home. In the splendour of his garage, planning and executing are merged, the work process is fully under his control. Work becomes a part of life.

The degradation of skilled work, of course, is occurring at a varying pace and in a different manner, depending on the industry or the trade. Where it occurs, it is usually not accepted passively by skilled workers. Whether in countless on-the-job struggles or in their unions, skilled workers are often the most vocal and best organized in their discontent, even though, compared to production workers they clearly have the best jobs at the highest rates of pay.

On the surface, the solution would appear to be to make skilled work more meaningful by reversing the trend towards more compartmentalized work and giving workers more say about how to do their jobs. But, this would put management at the mercy of the independence of its workers. It would cost them money, and companies are not in business to provide hospitable work environments, but to maximize profits.

Even more importantly, such reforms wouldn't begin to tap people's energies fully. Restoring some independence to skilled work would improve the job, but it would not challenge the relation of the worker to the work process, nor alter the basic nature of that process itself. Instead workers should decide *what* is to be done as well as *how* it should be done. Without this, the basic framework remains: the manager is the trainer and the worker is the horse. True, there are trainers who beat their horses and trainers who give carrots to their horses. There may even be trainers who eat with their horses, but I have never seen a horse ride a trainer. What we must do is eliminate the relation of trainer to horse among humans.

The same dynamic to maximize profits that has caused skilled work to become fragmented has caused some managers to investigate the widening of production work. The motivation is rather clear: production workers who have become aware of other possibilities in life besides dull, repetitive, meaningless work often manifest their discontent with sabotage, absenteeism, wildcat strikes and shoddy workmanship The same worker who on Thursday appears to be satisfied with his job, may not even be at his work bench on Friday or Monday.

Even at best, job enrichment is sold on the basis that increased "participation" will result in increased productivity. J.M. Roscow of the *Work in America Institute,* referring to proponents of job enrichment, said: 'Their overriding concern—like Ford's— is productivity. But . . . it's their belief that job satisfaction . . . higher quality of working life . . . will not only make for more loyal, satisfied employees, but will actually *increase* productivity.'

There is a strong élitism that runs through many if not all of these plans: they produce jobs that are not inherently interesting, but only interesting "for workers". I have never heard of a job enrichment professional being so taken with the result of his efforts that he decided to stay on that job after "enriching" it, and himself actually producing mirrors, dog food, or what have you.

Workers try to retain their humanity by escaping from the production process; job enrichment instead tries to further integrate them into essentially uninteresting work. Job enrichment plans assume that, when a worker puts in a dozen different kinds of bolts rather than the same one twelve times, the work is inherently more satisfying. Often the result is twelve boring jobs instead of one.

I asked a friend in Detroit who works in the pits (under the assembly line) what he thought of the Volvo plant where the cars are turned on their sides and work in the pits is eliminated. He was opposed to this idea because he had devised a way to do his timed operation in 30 seconds instead of 56 seconds and could therefore sit down out of sight when he was done. If he had been above ground, his additional 30 seconds would have been quickly "enriched". What does this say about a society where workers are opposed to coming above ground at the workplace?

In order to encourage workers to come out of the pits, job enrichment programmes promise not only better working conditions, but "new horizons for work". While the nature of work remains fundamentally unaltered, the prophets of these programmes manage to pervert the language we use to talk about work. It is not enough to talk about making some jobs more tolerable; instead we are offered a "new world of work", "democratizing the work place", and "dignity and freedom".

Michael Maccoby, director of the Harvard Project on Technology, Work and Character, and also director of an experimental programme between Harman Industries and the UAW illustrates this new use of language. He speaks of four principles being the key to the programme: security, equity, democracy and individuation.

I would like to examine two of these concepts: democracy and individuation. Democracy is defined by Maccoby as 'giving each worker more opportunities to have a say in the decisions that affect his life'. This is an insult to workers and to language. Democracy is not having *a* say, it is having *the* say. Counterposed to Maccoby, the dictionary defines democracy as 'government in which the people hold the ruling power either directly or through elected representatives'. In all kinds of authoritarian systems workers have *a* say, but we would hardly call that democracy. Even in the ante-bellum South, slaves had certain rights and a limited control over the work they did. The question is, in case of conflict between democratic trappings and authoritarian control, which wins? While "job enrichment" might strengthen or even add democratic elements to the work place, its purpose is to make the fundamentally authoritarian organization easier to manage, not to make it basically democratic. What we are left with is a new definition of democracy for the work place: workers make no basic decisions, instead they have *a* say.

Individuation supposedly 'expresses the goal of stimulating the fullest possible development of each individual's creative potential'. A statement this sweeping is nonsense as long as we can even consider the primary definition of a person as a worker. If this can be accomplished within the work place it could only mean that people have limited potential. I reject that. People will only begin to fully realize their "creative potential" when work ceases to be a separate and compartamentalized part of life. They certainly won't do it manufacturing mirrors for Cadillacs, the product made by Harman.

Some specific improvements that come out of a job enrichment programme can undoubtedly improve the job. However, they certainly do not change the character of work, which is what I believe must be done. In industrial society work is a prison. No doubt any prisoner would prefer being at a minimum security prison like Allenwood (where the Watergate criminals were sent), which would be akin to a benign capitalist system rather than a hell-hole like Leavenworth, the equivalent of a labour camp. But both remain prisons.

We define an institution as a prison when it incarcerates people, regardless of how pleasant the confinement might be. In the same way, when labour power is sold under capitalism, work becomes separate from life even though a certain flexibility might be conceded for efficient production.

In order to change the character of work, we cannot just look at the work place but we have to focus on the nature of the larger society. The limits of focusing on the work place were made comically clear by Dr. Robert N. Ford, personnel director for manpower utilization of the American Telephone and Telegraph Company, in Senate hearings on worker alienation in 1972. Dr. Ford glowingly described the benefits of increased employee control over their work. So-called "customer service representatives" were given the right, without any consultation with superiors, to set credit ratings for customers, ask for, and determine the size of a deposit, and cut off a customer's service for non-payment. When an autoworker's telephone is cut off, it will be of little comfort for him to know that a phone worker somewhere is enjoying the increased responsibility of an enriched job. Unfortunately, Dr. Ford will not be around to hear the autoworker's response.

Beyond the phone company, it is not enough for us to talk about humanizing the strip mining that destroys the environment, or manufacturing napalm in a more creative way, or building a frightening eleven million cars a year with teams rather than on assembly lines. It is not enough to question how we produce, if we neglect to consider *what* we produce, and the *uses* of that production. Is it too much to demand an enquiry into the ethics of industrial production?

The reward for enduring work under capitalism is called leisure. Those who do not work on assembly lines, or coke ovens, or in machine shops remind those who do, that while one half or more of a worker's waking hours might be boring and meaningless, his leisure and retirement will be fulfilling.

Clark Kerr, former chancellor of the University of California, expressed this sentiment almost poetically:

> 'The great new freedom may come in the leisure time of individuals. Higher standards of living, more free time and more education make this not only possible but almost inevitable. Leisure will be the happy hunting ground for the independent spirit . . . The economic system may be highly ordered and the political system barren ideologically; but the social

and recreational and cultural aspects of life should be quite diverse and quite changing.'

Rather than leisure being the "happy hunting ground for the independent spirit", it is degraded by the same forces that degrade work. Enforced leisure or retirement is not so much a jubilee as it is a parole whose quality has already been determined by the sentence served. On one level, the frustration and tension of the job are not easily left behind at the plant gate. Leisure becomes a frenzied managed activity to forget the job rather than a satisfying experience.

On a more basic level, the fragmented nature of life under capitalism and the intense drive of the system to sell what it produces lead us to seek satisfaction in commodities rather than in what we can do for ourselves. Leisure becomes an industry rather than a pursuit, providing us with more "efficient" alternatives for relaxation.

If we simply take a walk in the forest it may be pleasurable, but it does little to raise our "standard of living". Instead, if we drive monstrous campers into camping grounds that are little different from housing estates, entire industries are created. Industries not just to manufacture campers, but to produce portable refrigerators, stoves, bathrooms, televisions. We certainly don't have to worry about walking, because other industries come into being to provide exercise for us—figure salons, diet foods, etc. Even our dogs no longer have to exercise: diet dog foods are available to meet their "needs".

At each step of the way, we require increasing numbers of experts to repair our campers, trim our bodies, recommend food for our dogs, and relax our minds. What industrial society gives us is the ultimate professionalism: armies of experts determining and having the weapons of manipulation to enforce our "needs". After our "needs" are determined, one possibility only is offered to satisfy them: remain in the system and produce. Culture becomes the outer wall of the prison that is work. The system that makes work meaningless makes life meaningless: both reflect the drives of the society.

The central drive, production for profit, is incompatible with humanizing the society. We are told that production for profits is the only efficient way to provide us with a decent and satisfying life, yet at best, a relatively high standard of consumption has become far different from a fulfilling life. To produce this consumption requires that the vast majority of us remain as horses, and let's face it, there are limits to the satisfactions and visions a horse can have of life. Discussions about improving work become essentially discourses on how the trainer can best harness the horse.

In order to free the productive activity of man and leisure from this subordination, the social relations in the society must be radically altered. I propose a full and democratic workers' control of not only the work place but also of the society as a means to transform the nature of work and leisure in the most fundamental way. This demands a revolutionary change in society, confronting the industrial system, the state and all its institutions. Revolution, however, is not the solution: it is the condition that makes solutions possible. Workers' control is the first step to eliminate work as a separate and alien part of our lives and thereby humanize the society. In the process, we should re-examine the use of industrial production as we know it.

As a skilled worker, I don't just want to control the present industrial system and the culture it has defecated. I want workers' control for a new and better society. It will be a victory for us, as workers, to democratically run industry, but it does not constitute a victory for us as men. It will be a triumph for man when we begin to cultivate new life styles based on a complete inversion of our present society. The entire monstrous edifice of relations of the production of goods can't be merely taken over: it was brutally built with the needs of the present owners and managers in mind. We will have to lay new cornerstones and build on new human and humane foundations.

Perhaps this will enable us to regain those human functions that have been taken from us. Extra-ordinary dreams may become everyday reality. Today some of us have hopes of building these life styles within capitalist society. To the extent that this is possible it amounts to a few going over the prison wall, becoming the proverbial drop-outs, often to live dependent on the output of those that remain. If only a few make it, they may be tolerated. If too many attempt to escape all will be forced back. The only real alternative is to tear down the walls and abolish the institutions that imprison us. To paraphrase Eugene Debs' words of half a century ago: if a soul remains in prison, none of us are free.

Instead of going over the wall or attempting to

run our work-prisons co-operatively within capitalism, workers' control is the first step towards building a system that will allow people to determine and fulfil their real needs. The inspiration of skilled workers who never fully resigned themselves to being only "hands" or "horses" may contribute to the replacement of industrial society, capitalist or otherwise, with one that will not separate work from life and thus impoverish both. For all of us, this will be a celebration of life.